D0997431

# ONE HUNDRED AND ONE THINGS
## TO DO IN WAR TIME
### 1940

## Foreword by the Publisher

In business since the 1840s, B T Batsford was a well-established London publishing house as World War II broke out. Fearful of losing books and staff in the London bombing, the company adjourned to a Malvern countryside villa, but kept an eye on the London office. As Harry Batsford said: 'As the war has scattered authors, printers and photographers all over the country, it is just as easy to handle them from the Malvern slopes as from Mayfair.'

*101 Things to Do in Wartime* (published 1940) was one of the many books that Batsford published during the war. It was part of the long-running and much-loved 101 Things series, which started in the 1920s and included *101 Things for Little Folk to Do, 101 Things for a Boy to Make, 101 Games to Make and Play* and *101 Things for the Housewife to Do.* The authors of many of the books in the series, Lillie B. Horth and husband Arthur C. Horth, between them helped foster the British crafting tradition. During the war, their good-natured, no-nonsense practical advice was ideally suited to the wartime effort at home. Whether you were after waterless cooking recipes or games to play with the children during the blackout, the Horths had the answers.

Reading through these pages again, I am struck by the soundness of so much of the advice more than 60 years on and more specifically how its emphasis on conservation and recycling is now a 21st-century necessity. Similarly, their advice on ensuring exercise and good nutrition for children could be written today, although perhaps not in quite so charming a way. The book deserves to be back in print – exactly as it was in 1940 – for so many reasons. But, for me, the sense of a bygone era and the charm of the phrasing and language is what I enjoy the most. It reflects so much of what has changed in generations but also so much of what endures from an era of make-do-and-mend and sacrifice.

Publisher, B T Batsford 2007

SIMPLE RUG DESIGNS.

# 101 THINGS TO DO IN WAR TIME
# 1940

## A PRACTICAL HANDBOOK
## FOR THE HOME

BY

## LILLIE B. & ARTHUR C. HORTH

LONDON
B. T. BATSFORD, LTD.

First Published, Spring 1940
Reprinted Autumn 2007

By B T Batsford
The Old Magistrates Court
10 Southcombe Street
London W14 0RA

An imprint of Anova Books Company Ltd

Volume copyright © Batsford

The moral right of the authors has been asserted.

All rights reserved. No part of this publication may be reproduced,
stored in a retrieval system, or transmitted in any form or by any
means electronic, mechanical, photocopying, recording or
otherwise, without the prior written permission of the copyright
owner.

ISBN- 9780713490572

A CIP catalogue record for this book is available from the British
Library.

15 14 13 12 10 09 08 07
10 9 8 7 6 5 4 3 2

Printed by SNP Leefung Printers Ltd, China

This book can be ordered direct from the publisher at the website:
www.anovabooks.com, or try your local bookshop.

# PREFACE

WAR TIME has brought with it many problems for the householder and housewife to solve, many of them new and most of them presenting difficulties. In compiling this volume of " 101 Things to Do," we have selected some of the more important of these problems in the hope that they help in providing suggestions for exercising greater economies in various directions, and also in ideas for utilising in some practical way the long hours of the black-out.

In the previous books on " 101 Things to Do," practical suggestions have been given for suitable occupations for every member of the family, including Little Folks, the Boy, the Girl, the Handyman and the Housewife. They all contain some help most needed at the present time. In this new " 101 Things to Do," special attention is given to economy in food, cooking, fuel and light ; the special problems dealing with the black-out and evacuees, and the provision of extra food supplies, such as garden produce, mushrooms, eggs, poultry, rabbits and honey.

A considerable number of pages are devoted to indoor amusements, recreations and occupations. Instructions are given for making Puppets, and the necessary apparatus for many table and floor games. Craft articles include leatherwork, patchwork and appliqué, rug-making and knitting, suitable for the Services as well as for personal use. For the children there are round games, methods of dressing dolls and several kinds of toys. For emergencies there is a section on First Aid and bandaging.

L. B. AND A. C. HORTH.

WORTHING.

# ACKNOWLEDGMENT

THE Authors and Publishers have pleasure in recording their grateful thanks to the following, who have so kindly given permission and placed at their disposal the materials necessary for the reproduction of the illustrations :

The British Mushroom Industry, Ltd., Plate XXIII ; Messrs. Corfield-Sigg, Ltd., Plate XXXI ; The Dennison Manufacturing Co., Ltd., Plates I, V, VI (lower subject), IX ; The Dryad Press, Plates II (top subject from " Dressed Soft Toys," by E. Moody, and the lower subject from " Cut Woolly Toys," by E. Mochre and I. P. Roseaman), III and IV (from " The Making of Soft Toys," by C. Elliot Eldman), VIII and XXV (from " Constructive Knitting," by Olive Hacking), XIII, XIV (from " The Craft of Model Making," by Thomas Bayley, R.B.A.) ; The Excell-o-Ribbon Co., VI, VII ; Messrs. George Lee & Sons, Ltd., XV, XVI ; Messrs. Patons & Baldwins, Ltd., Frontispiece, XVII, XVIII, XIX, XXVI, XXVII, XXX, XXXV ; Studiette Handcrafts, Messrs. Christopher Webb, Ltd., XI, XII ; Messrs. Windolite, Ltd., XXXIV ; Messrs. George Newnes & Co., Ltd., and Messrs. Weldons, Ltd., for subjects which have appeared in their periodicals ; and William E. Bradford and Messrs. George Allen & Unwin, Ltd., author and publishers, respectively, of the handbooks " The Roller Bandage " and " First Aid Bandaging."

# CONTENTS

# CONTENTS

# INDOOR GAMES AND AMUSEMENTS

There are so many card and table games that it would be difficult to enumerate them all. Chess, draughts and dominoes as well as bridge, whist and other games played with playing cards have their enthusiasts and can be relied upon for pleasantly passing away the long hours of black-out. Several table and floor games are mentioned in these pages, together with instructions for making the apparatus. Many simple table games, used with counters and dice, can be obtained for the amusement of the younger members of the family as well as such old games as snap and the more modern lexicon, to mention only two.

However interesting and popular a game becomes, it is liable to become wearisome if carried on too long. With a small family there is likely to be no difficulty as the range of suitable games is so wide that frequent change is easy. When, however, a number of adults and also children are gathered together, it is often necessary to devise round games in which the grown-ups or children, separately or together, can be amused. There are round games in which everybody can join and others where one or more of the company entertains the rest. Most of these games are well known, but it often happens that they cannot be brought to mind just when they are needed ; the following brief reminders of just a few of the more popular will be helpful as suggestions for the hostess or organiser.

Acting games, such as Charades, Acting Proverbs, and Rhymes, the Farmyard, Tableaux Vivants, Comic Concerts, etc., are always popular. With Charades, Rhymes and Tableaux Vivants, there is no need for anything elaborate in the way of costume, much can be done with Dennison's crêpe paper and access to various wardrobes. Although a small stage is a help, two or three light screens suitably arranged will answer for the purpose, and if possible, they should be placed by the door so that the actors may use it for entrances and exits. Words of two or more syllables should be chosen, and the object generally is to make the word as ambiguous as possible. The choice of suitable words is not difficult, the following are suggestions—Arrowroot, Bellman, Bookworm, Champagne, Checkmate, Dovetail, Dustman, Ear-rings, Footman, Grandchild, Hardship, Illwill, Joyful, Kindred, Loophole, Matchless, Necklace, Outside, Painful, Quicklime, Roundhead, Season, Toadstool, Upright, Wedlock and Useful. Four-act words such as Craftsmanlike, Highwayman, Penmanship, Workmanship, etc., are much more difficult.

The game of acting rhymes consists of a word having a good many other words rhyming with it, chosen by the audience. The first player begins by silently acting some word that will rhyme with the one chosen. As each word is acted it should be guessed by the audience before the next one is attempted. For example, the word might be rose. The actor could pose, do some needlework, scatter seed, imitate rowing, shutting a door, or pulling down a blind.

The comic concert may be played in several ways, one is to arrange the actors in a row in front of the audience, with each member imitating the actors of an instrumentalist. Another way is to use one actor to do the imitations and let the audience write down the name of the instrument. The whole company can take part, a leader being supposed to furnish each member with an instrument and then he imitates in turn each instrument, the possessor of that instrument should then perform. Finally, he should conduct a concert with the whole of the instruments with or without the accompanying initated sounds. There are many variations of this amusing game. The farmyard is another example.

There is a multitude of round games in which all members of the party can take part. Among the more popular are Adjectives, in which the players write down half a dozen adjectives. One of the company tells a story and the story is re-told with the adjectives supplied substituted. Alphabet games consist of serving each member of the party with a number of letters and ask them to form a name as best they can. Exchanges in turn may be arranged on payment of a fine.

Blind Man's Bluff, Blowing out the Candle, Blowing the Feather, Blind Postman, Finding the Ring, Forfeits, Hunt the Slipper, Musical Chairs, The Minister's Cat, Oranges and Lemons, Postman's Knock, Spelling Bee, Simon Says, Stage Coach, This and That, What am I Doing? and Yes or No? are all well-known games.

Games with paper and pencil include Consequences, Crambo, Definitions, and Judge and Jury, are round games, popular at parties. Advertisements without wording, and Kim's game, are suitable for prizes, and should be prepared beforehand. The Donkey's tail and similar games are useful for children's parties. There should be no difficulty in finding suitable interests for the younger children and particularly those from seven years to eleven years old. In addition to the suggestions given above, very many more will be found in " 101 Things for Little Folks to Do." The children will find the coloured plates attractive and will be able to follow the simple instructions which are printed in large type. For girls there is " 101 Things for Girls to Do " and for boys " 101 Things for Boys to Make." These three books offer suitable amusements and occupation for all the younger members of the family. All are fully illustrated, and the descriptions are written in simple language to enable them to follow the instructions without help.

The popular game of Darts should not be forgotten; it is necessary to provide a good light for the board and the area surrounding the board should be suitably protected from mis-directed darts. Floor games such as Parlour Quoits, Skittles and Croquet, are easily arranged and, of course, table games like Billiards, Bagatelle and Ping-pong, Croquet are all suitable for the long winter evenings.

# A TABLE FOR PING-PONG

Table tennis or ping-pong is an ideal game for the long winter evenings, and although it is possible to play a game of sorts on a dining or kitchen table, it is more satisfactory to instal a full-size table. The normal size is 9 ft. by 5 ft., preferably in one piece ; if not, in two.

A single table with a suitable trestle is shown on the next page, it is made with one sheet of $\frac{3}{16}$ in. or $\frac{1}{4}$ in. thick plywood. The framework should be about 2 in. by $1\frac{1}{4}$ in., so that sufficient rigidity is ensured. Join the ends and the three cross rails to the side lengths with the lapped joint, and brad the plywood at intervals of 3 in. or 4 in. on all sides ; thin plywood should be bradded to the cross rails as well.

The trestle should be made from 2 in. by $1\frac{1}{4}$ in. wood. Prepare two 5 ft. 6 in. lengths for the top and two 5 ft. lengths for the lower tails. These are joined by 4 ft. lengths at the ends and 3 ft. 6 in. lengths between with approximately 3 ft. 6 in. lengths for the diagonal struts. All joints should be lapped, although the mortise and tenon joint is stronger. Join the two sets of legs with $\frac{1}{4}$ in. bolts with a thin washer between, and fit stout cord or webbing across about 6 in. away from the ends. All joints should be lapped. Join the two sets of legs with $\frac{1}{4}$ in. bolts with a thin washer between, and fit stout cord or webbing across about 6 in. away.

The underneath view and the side view of a table in two sections is shown at the bottom of the next page. The plywood should be 4 ft. square, bradded to a framework of $1\frac{1}{2}$ in. by $1\frac{1}{4}$ in. wood, with butt joints at the corners. The legs are made of the same material, four lengths for the uprights are 2 ft. $5\frac{3}{4}$ in., and two for the rails are 3 ft. $8\frac{1}{2}$ in. Join 6 in. or so down with the halving joint and brace with strips of $1\frac{1}{2}$ in. by $\frac{1}{2}$ in. wood. Insert pieces of $1\frac{1}{2}$ in. wood at opposite ends and screw up legs, provide spring stays on the outside of the legs to keep them in position.

4

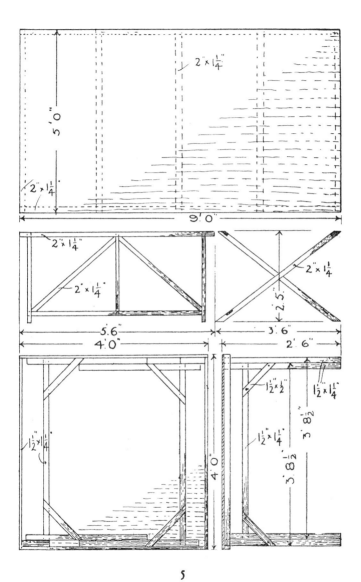

5

# TABLE TENNIS RACKETS AND
# NET SUPPORTS

The illustrations on the next page show methods for making table tennis or ping-pong rackets, and also the supports for the net, the material for the latter can be purchased or ordinary curtain net can be used. The bottom and top edges of the net, approximately 6 in. wide, are provided with a narrow border of white material, tape is suitable.

Plywood for the rackets should be $\frac{3}{16}$ in. thick, shaped to an ellipse, approximately 6 in. wide by $6\frac{1}{2}$ in. long, cut from a piece measuring $10\frac{3}{4}$ in. by 6 in. or so. The handle should be $1\frac{1}{4}$ in. wide. The shape can be cut out with a fret or padsaw, and the edges finished with a spokeshave. One side should be covered with No. o glasspaper, and the other with thin cork veneer. Use thin glue and place the wood under pressure until the glue has set. Cover the handles with sheet cork just over $\frac{1}{4}$ in. thick, glued on, the rounded surface can be shaped with a rasp and finished with a flat file. Drive in two brads each side when finished.

Cheap G cramps can be used to support the netting, one method is to use lengths of stout wire or iron rod which should be secured to the outside of each cramp with wire; a touch of solder would help to keep the binding firm. Another method is to bend some strip iron as shown at the bottom of the page. In this case it will be necessary to drill holes in the lower bend of the upright and the upper portion of the cramp, and rivet the two portions together. It will be necessary also to drill holes in the uprights so that the net can be tied in position. A coat of green paint or enamel would improve the appearance of the supports.

It should be noted that when the sectional table is used, it will be necessary to secure the two portions together; this can be done with hasps and staples.

6

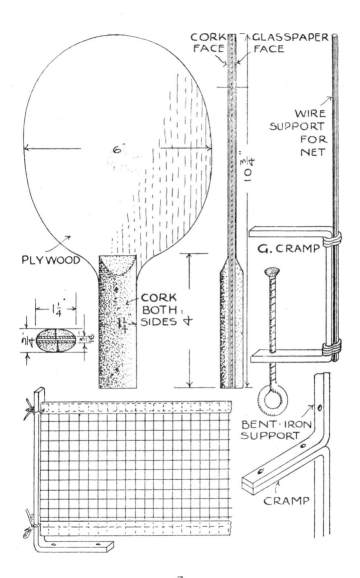

CORK FACE

GLASSPAPER FACE

WIRE SUPPORT FOR NET

$10\frac{3}{4}$"

6"

G. CRAMP

PLYWOOD

CORK BOTH SIDES

$1\frac{1}{4}$

$1\frac{1}{4}$

$\frac{3}{16}$

BENT·IRON SUPPORT

CRAMP

7

# CROQUET FOR THE TABLE AND THE FLOOR

A modified game of croquet can be played on a table or carpet as well as on a lawn. The size of a croquet lawn is 35 yd. by 28 yd., and, as far as possible, any modified game should be played on a surface having the same proportions; for example, a floor game 5 yd. by 4 yd., or a table space of 4 ft. 6 in. by 3 ft. 6 in. would do. The lay-out shown on the next page can be adapted to circumstances.

The floor game can be played with ordinary tennis balls and ping-pong balls for the table game. The hoops and mallets should be made to suit. Hoops are easily made from ¼ in. dia. iron rod for use on the floor, and with ⅛ in. dia. galvanised wire for the table. It will be seen that the hoops are supported by bottom extensions to form feet. One or two posts will be needed according to the game to be played, for floor use an 18 in. length of broomstick should be screwed to a 6 in. circle of zinc or stout tinned sheet. Dowel rod of ¼ in. diameter, mounted on a tin disc, will do for the table.

Mallets for floor use may be made from lengths of old wooden curtain rails or any round wood about 2½ in. dia., but equally effective heads can be made from short lengths of stout postal tube filled in with cork or wood discs. The diagram on the next page gives a section of a suitable head. The core should be glued in securely and should be strong enough to stand up to the work required. Handles, approximately 33 in. long, may be either lengths of dowelling or bamboo; if the latter material is used the inside should be plugged at the end so that a screw can be driven in from the outside of the head. The mallets for table croquet can be made from suitable dowelling to the sizes given. In both games the ordinary rules of croquet should be followed.

8

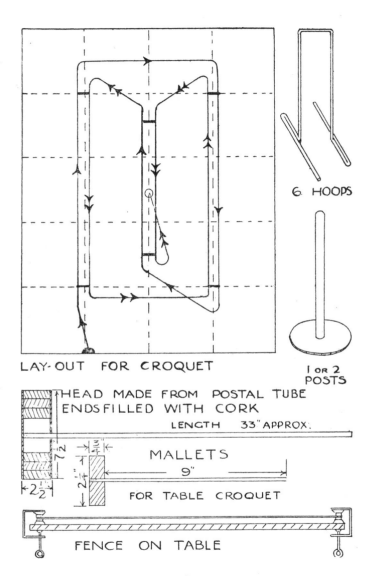

LAY-OUT FOR CROQUET

6. HOOPS

1 OR 2 POSTS

HEAD MADE FROM POSTAL TUBE ENDS FILLED WITH CORK
LENGTH 33" APPROX.

MALLETS

9"

FOR TABLE CROQUET

FENCE ON TABLE

# EASILY MADE PIN TABLE

The form of table bagatelle, known as a pin table, is somewhat expensive to buy but not at all difficult to make. The diagram on the next page gives all the essential dimensions as well as the various scoring points. The base is made from a piece of $\frac{3}{8}$ in. thick plywood with thin plywood for the rim.

Prepare the base to 29$\frac{3}{4}$ in. by 13$\frac{3}{4}$ in., mark off a semicircle at the top and finish the edges square to the face. Set off the lines for the circles and holes, etc., and outline them with pencil. Provide some brass tubing having an inside diameter of $\frac{9}{16}$ in. and cut off $\frac{1}{8}$ in. rings. Find a centre bit to cut a hole equal to the outside diameter of the tube and bore holes just over $\frac{1}{8}$ in. deep. Fit in a ring to each of the eleven holes. Drill a fine hole, not more than $\frac{1}{4}$ in. deep and exactly $\frac{1}{8}$ in. behind each recess.

Space out the holes for the nails about $\frac{3}{16}$ in. apart, noting that the openings vary with the size of the circles. The set of three pins at the top of the top circles and those between the two lower circles should be $\frac{9}{16}$ in. apart. Provide a rubber stop as at S, this should project about $\frac{1}{4}$ in. Before proceeding further clean the whole of the surface with fine glasspaper.

The rim should be $\frac{1}{8}$ in. thick plywood, 1$\frac{1}{4}$ in. wide, it will bend sufficiently to allow it to be bradded over the curve, but if there is any difficulty, the inside of the bend can be scored with a sharp knife at equal spaces $\frac{1}{4}$ in. apart. If possible, the two sides and the top should be in one length. Prepare the strips for the bottom and the side A, fit a piece B, and then prepare the Cue, this can be made from dowel rod. Use $\frac{3}{4}$ in. or $\frac{7}{8}$ in. brads, and take particular care to drive them upright. The steel balls should be $\frac{9}{16}$ in. diameter, but marbles may be used.

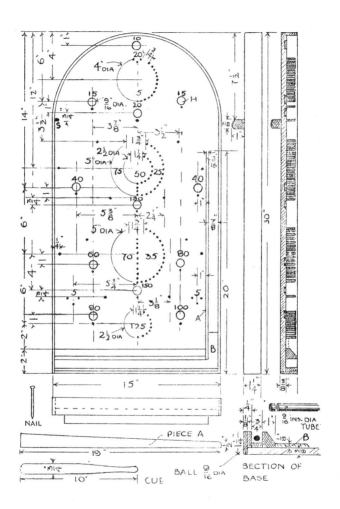

NAIL

PIECE A

19"

CUE

10"

BALL 9/16 DIA

SECTION OF BASE

15"

20

30"

9/16 INS. DIA TUBE

# A SIMPLE BALL GAME

The game shown on the next page is easily made with a piece of plywood, some short pieces of 2 in. by 1 in. batten, three wooden balls, a screw-eye and a few yards of elastic. First prepare a circular plate of plywood with a diameter from 12 in. to 14 in. Divide the circumference into five parts and inscribe an inner circle to give the centres of the five 1½ in. diameter openings; these can be made with an expanding centre bit, or with a 1 in. centre bit and a scribing gauge. A fretworker will have no difficulty in cutting out the holes.

The circular plate should be supported by two uprights, these should be cut from 2 in. by 1 in. wood to about 16 in. long. They should be let in a base of the same width and thickness to a depth of ½ in., leaving from ½ in. to ¾ in. between them, the latter being the width of a small G cramp used in attaching the base to a table. A separate view of the base portion is shown, this indicates the position of the two grooves for the uprights. The latter should be screwed or nailed securely to the base piece, the plywood plate should be screwed to the two front edges of the uprights. The screw-eye should be placed in the centre of the plate. The position of the G cramp is shown in the side view.

The balls should not be more than 1¼ in. diameter, otherwise it will be too difficult to get them into the holes. The rubber should be about 18 in. long and each of the three balls should be attached very securely, a hole being drilled in each one and the rubber knotted on the outside. The holes in the plywood disc may be numbered as shown. A variation of the game may be arranged by having the numbers on a disc of cardboard which can be moved round at will, or a block of wood can be inserted between the uprights at the back and the circular disc attached with one centre screw to allow of movement.

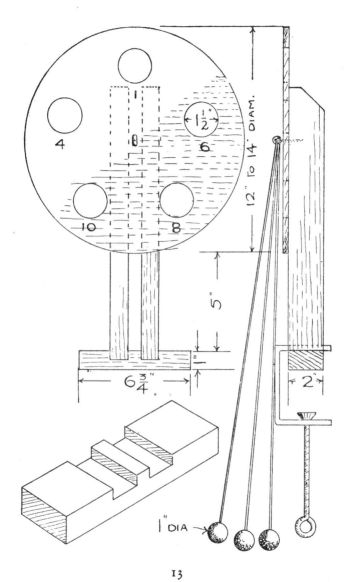

4

1

0

$1\frac{1}{2}''$

6

10

8

12" TO 14" DIAM.

5"

1"

$6\frac{3}{4}''$

2"

1" DIA

# BALANCING TOYS

Considerable entertainment can be obtained in making as well as from the action, of balancing toys, they can be made from thin fretwood or plywood with a fretsaw, and with the help of either poster colours or various enamel paints, the colouring can be carried out to produce decorative articles.

A simple form of balancing is shown at Fig. 1, and a number of different forms may be made on the same principle. The shape is drawn out to a larger scale at Fig. 2, it can be reproduced quite easily on a piece of plywood ruled out in squares. It is suggested that a piece of wood, 10 in. by 6 in., should be used, and the bottom circle made to 1 in. diameter. The parrot-shape lends itself to brilliant colouring. It will be sufficient for a suitable balance to glue 1 in. diameter blocks on each side of the bottom circle, as shown at Fig. 3.

The bird-shape, shown at Fig. 4, is arranged on a different form of balance, a small disc of sheet lead or a suitable casting in the same metal is attached to a length of stiff brass or galvanised wire fitted to the base of the toy. All sorts of shapes can be balanced in the same way, providing that the foot is suitably rounded.

Instead of a balance weight, the parrot-shape can be provided with a short length of dowel rod passed through a hole in the position indicated by P. The projecting dowel should be supported on parallel bars as suggested at Fig. 5. In the latter case, a clown has been substituted for the parrot. Another method of dealing with the balancing toy is to attach the weight at the bottom of the shape. For example, the bird at Fig. 4 can be made with the body in one piece, and the leg and wing shape made in duplicate and glued to the body shape, as at Fig. 6. In this case the weight should be fitted between the feet, as at W. The required shape can be made by bending a strip of tin and forming a mould to take some molten lead.

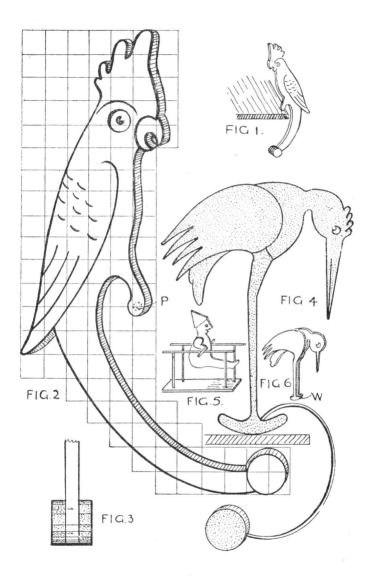

FIG 1.

FIG.2

FIG.3

P

FIG.5.

FIG 4

FIG 6

W

# HOME-MADE WORKING TOYS

There are numbers of small working toys quite easily made from odds and ends of wood, two typical examples being shown on page 17. The actual dimensions of each example may be related to the size of the available material, but in order to indicate a suitable proportion, the shapes are shown enclosed in squared lines to be reproduced to any desired size.

The top example consists of an animal shape, it can be a cat, dog, duck or anything else instead of the rabbit illustrated. The shape should be cut from plywood or thicker wood, if desired, and either let in or screwed on a grooved baseboard. A suitable size for the base is 6 in. by 2 in. by $\frac{1}{2}$ in. The wheels should be about 1 in. dia., and $\frac{1}{4}$ in. thick, they can be cut from a length of broomstick or adapted from cotton reels and attached with screws to axle blocks about $\frac{1}{2}$ in. by $\frac{1}{2}$ in. in section.

The moving chicken consists of eight parts, A represents the body, which is made in duplicate to any suitable size. The pieces B, C and D are shapes to fit between the pieces A. The head and neck are in one piece E, and the tail is shaped as at F. In fitting the parts together, the head and tail pieces are pivoted as indicated, pins being driven in as shown at P. When assembled, the pivoted portions are loose, the two sides of the body being glued and bradded to the small pieces, B, C and D.

The toy can be finished as a balancing toy by providing a base as shown, and attaching strings to the pins, the ends of the strings being tied to a small lead weight. Another method is to weight the bottom of the pieces E and F with a small strip of lead, so that they balance, and then to mount the chicken on a base with wheels similar to the rabbit. Finish the toys with paint or enamel.

PLATE I

NOVELTY DOLLS DRESSED WITH DENNISON CRÊPE.

PLATE II

CUT WOOLLY TOYS.

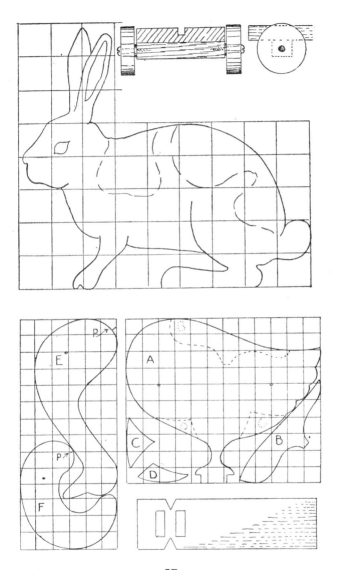

# PUZZLES IN CARDBOARD

Although all the puzzles shown on the next page can be cut out of thin plywood, they are more easily cut from cardboard with a sharp knife. The actual dimensions do not matter, but in each case the marking out should be accurate. The parts of each puzzle should be shuffled up and the problem is to arrange them in the original order as shown in the diagrams.

The octagon puzzle at Fig. 1 is marked out by first constructing a true octagon from a square by setting out the sides as shown by the dotted lines. The B spaces are parallel to the corners and drawn about two-fifths along, the position of the other divisions is clear.

The cross puzzle at Fig. 2 consists of five pieces, three are shaped as indicated at 1, the others are slightly different in length as at 2 and 3. The total length of the rectangle to begin with should be about one and a half times the width. The width of the cross pieces should equal the top, and the turns on all the ends should be square as indicated by the dotted lines.

The square puzzle at Fig. 3 is quite simple, although many people find it difficult to solve. It is essential that the squares and triangles should be cut out accurately. First set out the square to any desired size and divide into four equal parts, as shown by the dotted lines. Draw the diagonals and then join the corners of the four smaller squares. Cut along the lines to give three whole squares as at 1, 2 and 3, and ten triangles, as at 4 to 13.

There are many variations of these mechanical puzzles, for example, both the octagon and the square can be divided up in several different ways. It is understood that the numbering shown on the diagrams is omitted in making the puzzles, they are given to show how the pieces are fitted together.

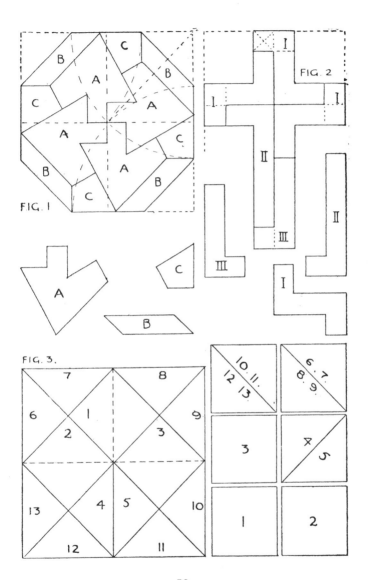

FIG. 1

FIG. 2

FIG. 3.

19

# PUZZLES IN WOOD

The block puzzle shown at Fig. 1 can be made with cubes about $1\frac{3}{4}$ in. by $1\frac{1}{4}$ in. by $1\frac{1}{4}$ in., or with blocks $1\frac{1}{4}$ in. by $1\frac{1}{4}$ in. by $\frac{3}{4}$ in., or so. They should be fitted in a case measuring 5 in. by 5 in. inside measurement with a border of either 1 in. or $\frac{3}{4}$ in. by $\frac{1}{4}$ in., and a base of $\frac{1}{4}$ in. thick plywood. The corners of the case may be mitred, butted or dovetailed. Each of the blocks should be numbered from 0 to 15, either painted or stencilled, but the better method is to cut the numbers with a V or parting tool, as shown in the separate detail. The keen woodworker may like to embellish the puzzle by making a more ornamental case, but in any case the blocks as well as the case should be painted or stained. An effective treatment is to use Colron or Varnene for the case and ebony stain for the blocks ; stencilling can be done in colour, or, if incised, the cuts can be filled in with coloured enamel.

The method of solving the puzzle consists in removing the block numbered 0 first and moving the pieces inside the case without taking them out so that they are reversed and No. 15 takes the place of No. 1. Other methods consist of taking out Nos. 0 and 15, place No. 15 in the place of No. 1 and No. 1 in the place of 15, and then replace in the original order without lifting up any block. The whole of the blocks can be placed in any order, the No. 0 block removed and the others arranged by single moves to the correct sequence 1 to 15, the No. 0 being replaced last of all.

The notch puzzles should be made from $\frac{1}{2}$ in. by $\frac{1}{2}$ in. wood and notched with a knife or chisel, as indicated. Sycamore, beech or holly are preferable to a soft wood in making the puzzle. The notches must be accurately set out and cut with a very sharp chisel. The puzzle should be put together by placing two B pieces together and then fitting in a C piece. The plain piece is inserted last of all.

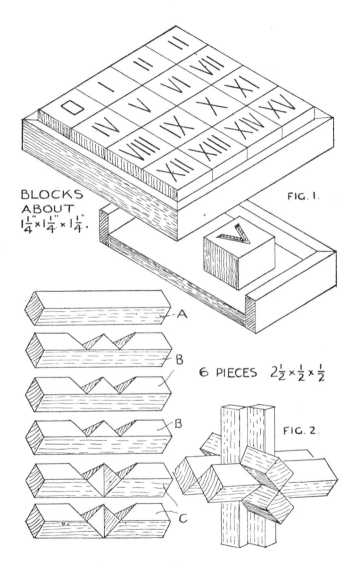

BLOCKS
ABOUT
$1\frac{1}{4}" \times 1\frac{1}{4}" \times 1\frac{1}{4}".$

FIG. 1.

A

B

B

C

6 PIECES $2\frac{1}{2} \times \frac{1}{2} \times \frac{1}{2}$

FIG. 2.

# WIRE PUZZLES

Wire puzzles provide interesting occupation not only for the solver but also for the maker. With two or three feet of No. 18 hard brass wire, or even galvanised wire of similar gauge, all the puzzles shown on the next page can be made with the aid of pliers. Approximately the diagrams show the puzzles to half-size, but actual dimensions are not so important as shape and proportion.

The puzzle at Fig. 1 consists of three parts, one a heart-shaped ring, and two bars, each having looped ends. The method of solving the puzzle is shown at Fig. 2, and it will be seen that the loop inside the heart-shape should be small enough to pass through the loop in the bent bar. The puzzle shown at Fig. 3 consists of two large loops fastened together with a small ring between. The method of solving is shown in three stages at Figs. 4, 5 and 6.

In the gridiron puzzle, at Fig. 7, the upper portion should not be more than 1½ in. square. To solve, remove the small ring from the centre portion by folding the latter so that the ring can be worked over the bars in the top portion. A simpler form of the same form of puzzle is shown at Fig. 8, with the method of solution at Fig. 9.

The bar puzzle shown at Fig. 10 consists of two rings on the ends of the horizontal bar, just too large to pull through the opening, the only way to remove the bar is to allow it to revolve down the double twist to the opening below. First fold the wire to a plain hairpin shape, place a short length of the wire between the two ends and twist a spiral turn for several rounds. The space left by the removal of the wire will leave sufficient room for the bar. The puzzle at Fig. 11 consists of working the ring from two to one spiral rounds, as shown by the dotted ring.

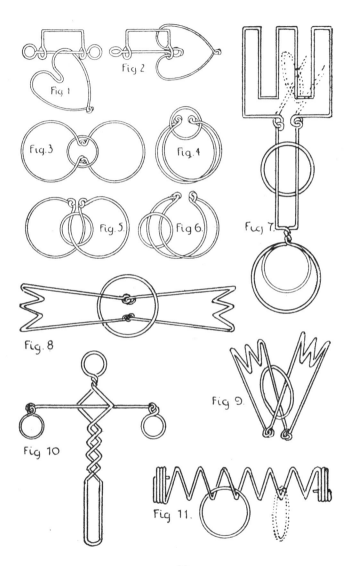

Fig 1

Fig 2

Fig. 3

Fig. 4

Fig. 5

Fig 6.

Fig 7.

Fig. 8

Fig 9.

Fig 10

Fig 11.

23

# TOYS IN WOOL AND FELT

Wool, felt and many fabrics can be used in making toys for the babies and those little folks who are too young to make their own playthings. Everybody must be familiar with the wool ball made by winding multi-coloured wool on a semi-circular cardboard foundation. The same idea can be developed by making special shapes from cardboard, on which the wool is wound, and many suggestions are illustrated on Plate II. Another way of making woolly toys quickly and easily is to use specially made wool on a wire foundation (known as wool twist) and manipulate it into various shapes and sewing them together. Small toys can be made in the same way by using pipe-cleaners.

A beginning should be made by making the woolly ball as shown on Plate II and follow with a hedgehog or mouse made in semi-elliptical shapes. The larger toys are made in several parts, and are joined together. All sorts of wool can be used from odds and ends of rug wool to knitting remnants, depending on the size and other conditions. Full instructions for making the toys can be obtained from " Cut Woolly Toys " published by the Dryad Press, 2s. Methods of making toys with wool twist will be found in a 6d. Dryad Leaflet, No. 113.

Besides felt, other special fabrics are available for making the soft toys shown on Plate III. These include animal baize, a washable imitation fur, in thick, fluffy and curly pile; in cream piggy velvet and in fleecy, feathery and silky pile. The toys can be stuffed with kapoc, wadding, wood wool, wool flock, or rubberised fibre. These can be obtained from Dryad Handicrafts, St. Nicholas Street, Leicester.

Considerable interest can be given to soft toys by dressing them as shown on Plate II. Suggestions, with full-size patterns for making and dressing Mrs. Bear and baby, Larry Lamb, Susan Rabbit, etc., will be found in *Dressed Soft Toys*, published by the Dryad Press.

PLATE III

SOFT TOYS.

PLATE IV

SOFT TOYS.

# WARTIME READING

Individual taste in reading varies so greatly that any attempt to indicate a course of reading would prove a difficult task; it is, however, possible to give some suggestions that will help in developing new interests.

The progress of the war can be followed by listening to the news bulletins and by reading the newspapers, but it can be made more interesting by the use of maps. To be really useful, maps should be of large scale and those published by, to take one example, *The Times* newspaper, are excellent. Travel books dealing with war regions will help in giving a better understanding of the country and the peoples.

A fascinating course of reading is that dealing with our own country, not just historical works, but books about the beauties of the countryside, the villages; the old towns and cities; the churches, abbeys and cathedrals; the castles, inns and gardens, such are to be found in varied volumes in the British Heritage series published by Batsfords. The English Life series, the Everyday Life series and the Pilgrims series are full of interest.

An engrossing study is the history of one's own locality and if accompanied by home-made maps and scale models, many hours of leisure can be employed in a profitable manner. It is interesting to begin with a medieval period and incorporate a study of the general conditions of the times, from such books as Quennells' " Everyday Things in England," " The Life and Work of the English People throughout the Centuries." Later periods will help to make more real such reading as biography and history and the classic fiction of Dickens, Scott, Thackeray, etc. Highly interesting books are Cobbett's " Rural Rides," White's " Natural History of Selbourne," Evelyn's and Pepys' " Diaries," Lyell's " Antiquity of Man "; Baring Gould's and Pulbrook's works on old English Country life will provide a fund of information and are interesting reading in themselves.

# SIMPLE CRAFTS IN PAPER, ETC.

## FILET MATS (Plate V)

Materials required :

1 Fold Dennison crêpe in required colour.
1 No. o steel crochet hook.
1 Crêpe twister.

Cut the Dennison crêpe in ½ in. strips across the grain, and push one end through the twister. Draw through as described on the instruction label. Ch. 47. 1st row : Turn, d.c. in 8th ch. from needle. * ch. 2 skip 2, d.c. in next ; repeat from * to end, 14 holes in row. 2nd row : Turn, ch. 5 d.c. in 2nd d.c., ch. 2, d.c. in next ; make 2 d.c. in hole and d.c. in d.c., until 7 d.c. have been made ; 6 holes along row, 7 d.c., to holes to end. 3rd row : Ch. 5. All holes. 4th row : 3 holes, 4 d.c., 3 holes, 7 d.c., 5 holes to end. Follow the pattern from here, repeating the motifs.

## THE CAMPUS JACKET (Plate VI)

Materials required :

2 Folds Dennison crêpe No. 183 sand.
1 Fold Do. each Nos. 128 blue, 154 ruby.
1 Pair No. 4 knitting needles.
1 No. o steel crochet hook.  1 crêpe twister.

*Note*—Once across constitutes one row. 2 rows constitutes one ridge. These instructions are for size 34.

The knitting of various persons varies so much that these instructions will have to be modified somewhat if you knit either very loosely or very tightly.

Cut strips of Dennison sand Crêpe ½ in. wide across the grain, and draw through the twister as instructed on the label.

BACK : Cast on 60 sts., k. 24 ridges or approximately 6 ins. K. 2 together at each end for 10 ridges. With 40 sts. on needle k. 20 ridges. Slope the shoulder by knitting together the first 2 sts. and last 2 sts. of each

PLATE VI

CROCHETED HAT, EXCELL-O-RIBBON.

CAMPUS JACKET MADE FROM
DENNISON CRÊPE.

PLATE V

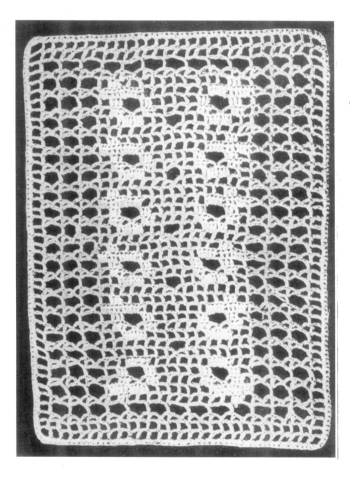

FILET TABLE MAT MADE FROM DENNISON CRÊPE.

row until 22 sts. remain in the centre.   Knit across and cast off.

FRONT : Make in 2 pieces.   Cast on 40 sts., k. 24 ridges.   For armhole cast off 5 sts. all on one row. Continue to cast off 1 st. at armhole edge of each ridge for 13 ridges.   Continue plain with 22 sts. on needle for 15 ridges.   At neck side cast off one st. on each ridge for 6 ridges.   Cast off one st. on each side until all sts. have been cast off.   The front, when finished, should have 5 more ridges in the armhole than the back.   Make 2 such pieces.

BAND : Knit separately and crochet to waist, blousing slightly.   Cast on 8 sts. in sand crêpe.   K. 30 ins. Crochet together shoulders and sides.   S.c. around edges with sand and then red, keeping armhole to size. To form button-holes on right edge, do not s.c. through previous row for 4 sts., instead ch. 4 with red.   Repeat at intervals for 5 button-holes.   S.c. around edges with sand, making 4 s.c. over chains.   D.c. edges with blue.   S.c. edges with sand.

## EXCELL-O HAT, BAG, AND BELT (Plates VI & VII)

Materials required :
>    3 Craft Reels Excell-O No. 227 black.
>    1 No. 0 steel crochet hook.

STITCH : S.c. taking up both loops of each stitch.

For crown ch. 3 and join in ring with sl. st.   Make 7 s.c. in ring, 2 s.c. in each s.c. on previous row.   Next row, increase every other st.   Cr. increasing sufficiently to keep work flat until circle measures $6\frac{3}{4}$ in. in diameter. Cr. without increasing until depth of crown measure $5\frac{1}{2}$ in. from top centre to edge.   For brim ch. tightly enough sts. to fit 22 in. head size when finished.   Work will draw up slightly as it is being crocheted.   Row 1 : start 2 sts. from hook and s.c. in each ch.   At this point measure head size.   If correct, join crocheted row with sl. st.   Row 2 : 1 s.c. in each s.c. of previous row.   Row

3 : increase every 5th st. Cr. in pattern for about 2½ in. increasing enough to keep work flat. Continue ½ in. without increasing. Have a crown and brim separately blocked, sew crown over ½ in. of brim, being sure right side of brim is next to face. Sew in 22 in. headband, and trim.

To make a bag to match the hat, crochet two circles in the same st. as that used for the hat. The circles must be kept perfectly flat, and should measure about 6 in. in diameter. If a larger or smaller bag is required, the circles must be made to size accordingly. Next cr. a strip 1¼ in. wide and long enough to go round ¾ of the circle's circumference in addition to the length of the handle, which is about 9 in. Fit this gusset between the circles, three-quarters of the way round, and the space left will form the opening of the bag. The loop which will be formed by the remainder of the strip makes the handle. Fold the ends of the handle towards the outside where they join the bag and stitch them. It will be found that the rest of the handle rolls round of its own accord. Next cr. a strip 2 in. long for the clasp. Stitch it at the centre on one side of the opening and bring it over the top. Fasten it on the other side with a button and loop. The belt is very simple to make. Cr. a long straight strip the required width and length, and sew a clasp buckle to the ends.

Glassip novelties are made by tying bundles of Glassips in the centre with wire and pulling the wire very tightly. This causes the Glassips automatically to spray outwards and form pom-poms. For a pom-pom made from full length Glassips, use 150 to 200 straws, and for smaller pom-poms, place rubber rings round the bundles and cut them down to the required length with scissors. To add to the effect, the Glassips can be tipped with coloured wax before being tied. Heat the end of a stick of wax over a spirit lamp until it melts and dab the melted end on to the end of the Glassip.

PLATE VII

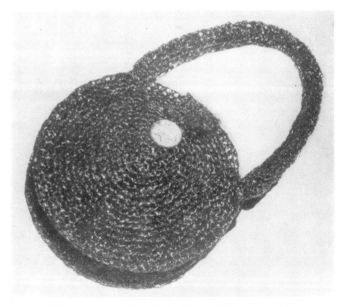

CROCHETED BELT AND HAND-BAG MADE FROM
EXCELL-O-RIBBON.

PLATE VIII

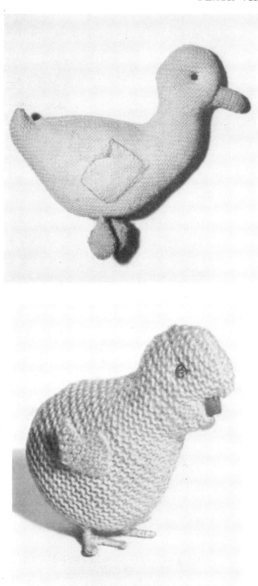

CHICKEN AND DUCKLING.

PLATE IX

SWEET PEAS AND CARNATIONS MADE FROM
DENNISON CRÊPE.

PLATE X

METHODS OF FOLDING CRÊPE PAPER FLOWERS.

## NOVELTY DOLLS (Plate I)

Novelty dolls are made from Dennison crêpe and wire. The head is a ball of crêpe, bound with a ½ in. strip of peach crêpe cut across the grain. It is then rolled in a square of the same colour, the grain of the crêpe going up and down on the head; this piece is gathered and fastened with wire at the top and bottom. The arms and legs are strips of wire looped at the ends, and wrapped with a strip of peach crêpe cut across the grain. Head arms and legs are then joined together and dressed as required, the doll's clothes being fastened with wire and paste.

## FLOWERS (Plates IX and X)

Realistic flowers can be made from Dennison crêpe paper and wire. The petals and leaves are first cut from pattern and then stretched and shaped with the fingers. The flowers are then assembled and fastened with wire, particular attention being given to the formation of each different type of flower. The photographs on Plate X show methods of shaping the petals and binding the wire stalks. Illustrations are given on Plate IX of carnations and sweet peas; these are only two of the many flowers to be made with Dennison's crêpe paper. Full instructions for cutting the shapes can be obtained from the Dennison Mfg. Co., Ltd., 52, Kingsway, London, W.C.2.

# BUILDING MODEL GALLEONS AND SHIPS

Of all forms of model making, galleons and ships are the most popular and certainly one of the most fascinating. The models may be records of the glorious episodes of the early explorers, of the fighting ships of the past and present, or may be small yachts and sailing ships for use on ponds and boating lakes. In each case it is an interesting and instructive occupation.

It would be a difficult task to collect all the necessary information required to build to scale one of the historic galleons or a replica of one of our modern fighting ships, but it is possible to obtain from the Studiette Handicrafts, Kent Street, Birmingham, a complete kit of parts with full instructions and full constructional details. The cost of the kits depend on the size and style of the model to be built ; they range from " Middy models " costing only a few shillings to larger and more ambitious pieces of construction costing £5.

The illustrations on Plates XI and XII give some indication of the appearance of the finished models which are designed true to scale and can be assembled by anyone using ordinary care. The kit contains the assembled hull with all masts, yards, sails, guns and innumerable other fittings, together with all information needed to complete the model.

The enthusiast who would like to build models from his own designs can obtain all sorts of metal and wood fittings from the above-mentioned firm ; these include sails, masts and rigging, guns and gun carriages, deck fittings and ready-made hulls.

Replicas of modern British fighting ships are obtainable in the form of water line models and include such well-known names as the Hood, Nelson, Rodney, etc. With waterline models it is possible to stage miniature naval engagements on the table or the floor, and it will not be difficult to make up all the small craft on similar lines.

PLATE XI

THE GOLDEN HIND.

H.M.S. VICTORY.

GALLEON MODELS MADE FROM
STUDIETTE KITS

PLATE XII

THE CUTTY SARK.

H.M.S. NELSON.

H.M.S. HOOD.

MODELS OF SHIPS MADE FROM
STUDIETTE KITS.

# PUPPETS AND PUPPETRY

The making and use of string and hand puppets offers fascinating occupation for the long evenings and helps to develop skill in manipulation. The presentation of a Marionette show will provide entertainment for the children as well as the grown-ups. The correct working of the puppets requires practise, but the art of puppetry is so fascinating that no trouble will be too much in attempting proficiency.

The puppets themselves are a source of great interest; they can be made quite easily by anyone with nimble fingers. There are many ways in which they can be constructed, two methods being illustrated on the next page. In one case, the foundation is built up with twisted wire with all the necessary joints, and the body, arm and leg shapes formed by covering the wire with gesso paste, made with glue and powdered whiting or by wrapping strips of paper or fabric, and by sewing up the shapes and stuffing them with kapoc. The other method is to use short lengths of dowel rod, the joints being made with screw-eyes. The head should be cut in wood or cork, or modelled in gesso or papier mâché.

The Dutch doll makes an excellent puppet, the joints should be altered and suitably hinged. Dressing is not easy but offers no great difficulty. It is better to have a number of puppets ready dressed for the parts rather than attempt to do much in the way of changing costumes. Puppets from 6 in. to 12 in. are controlled by strings attached to the body and limbs, and carried to two plain bars, but the most satisfactory method of control is that shown on the next page. The vertical rod is a 9 in. by ⅝ in. diameter dowel. The leg bar should be about the same length; this may be used separately or suspended on a hook at the top of the upright. Stiff brass wire should be fitted for the hand controls; in this case the string runs through the loops. The head is attached to strings fixed to a short bar fixed to the upright and

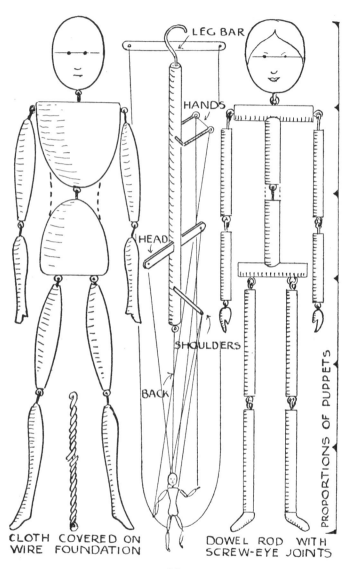

LEG BAR

HANDS

HEAD

SHOULDERS

BACK

CLOTH COVERED ON
WIRE FOUNDATION

DOWEL ROD WITH
SCREW-EYE JOINTS

PROPORTIONS OF PUPPETS

E

the shoulder strings are held by strings attached to the end of a length of wire or dowel, as indicated.

Hand puppets are made in the form of gloves as indicated on page 33. The head can be made of paper or shaped from wood, the neck should be hollow to take the first finger, and the hands of the puppet worked by the thumb and second finger.

The framework of a puppet theatre is shown on page 35; it consists of a simple framework covered by curtains. The height from the ground to the stage should be about 5 ft. 6 in., and the height of the proscenium about 2 ft., depending on the size of the puppets. A width from 3 ft. to 3 ft. 6 in. will be sufficient, and the depth may be from 1 ft. 10 in. to 2 ft. 6 in. Suitable scenery should be provided, this can be painted on stiff paper or canvas, using distemper, powder colours or poster paint. A wide shelf should be provided inside for the puppets when not in use. The stage should be well illuminated, a direct beam from a hanging electric light directed on the stage is quite satisfactory, but it is not a difficult matter to arrange foot-lights attached to a flex from the nearest point. As a rule lighting should be from the front to prevent undue prominence being given to the strings.

The dramatic side of puppetry provides unlimited opportunity for producing fairy tales, and even pantomimes, episodes from history, plays written for children, as well as for adults, are within the scope of the marionette theatre. One very great favourite is Punch and Judy, although this is more easily performed by the use of hand puppets. As the subject has great possibilities, the reader is advised to obtain a copy of " Hand Puppets and String Puppets," published by the Dryad Press at 2s. 6d., or " Puppetry at Home," by W. H. Whanslaw (Nelson). All materials for puppetry can be obtained from the Dryad Handicrafts, of St. Nicholas Street, Leicester.

PLATE XIII

PUPPETS MADE BY CHILDREN.

PLATE XIV

MODEL OF RUISLIP VILLAGE.

MODEL OF AN INTERIOR.

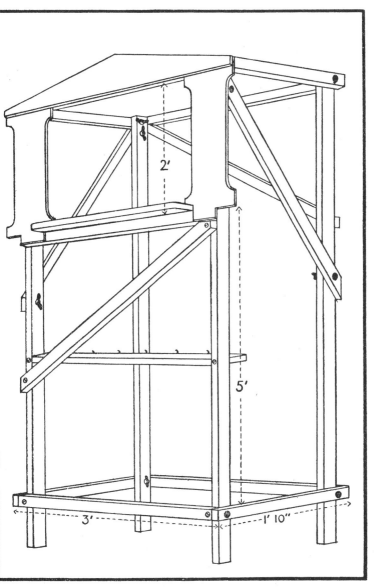

FRAMEWORK OF PUPPET THEATRE.

# MODELLING IN CARDBOARD

Of interest to adults as well as children, cardboard modelling offers a fine scope for the development of skill and ingenuity. Old cardboard boxes and odd pieces of strawboard, a pair of scissors and a penknife, a 12 in. ruler and a tube of seccotine or other adhesive, form the necessary equipment. Colouring can be done with poster or showcard colours. Samples of wall-paper, odd pieces of fabric, pieces of cork and plywood, and innumerable odds and ends can be put to good use by the model maker.

Some suggestions are given on the next page for elementary work, these should be made in order to obtain a good idea of the general method of work and followed by some definite scheme of work. For example, it would not be difficult to make a scale model of a small cottage or bungalow, and then proceed with the modelling of a village. Given time, the complete planning of a garden city would provide for highly interesting work.

The example at A is a typical small building. The lay-out or development of the construction is shown at B, the dotted lines show the position of the bends for the sides as well as the flanges. The crease for the bending should be done with the point of the scissors or with a bone folder. The folded model, ready for the roof and base, is shown at C, the lay-out for the roof is shown at D. The sentry box at E is similarly made.

A small house or cottage, as indicated at F, is made similarly to C, with a lay-out as shown at G. The windows can be painted on or cut out. An ordinary sloping roof, similar to A, can be fitted by cutting to the shape of the dotted lines, the lay-out for the roof of the model at F is shown at H. The eaves are at " a " and the slope of the roof is at " b." Elaboration as at K is simple.

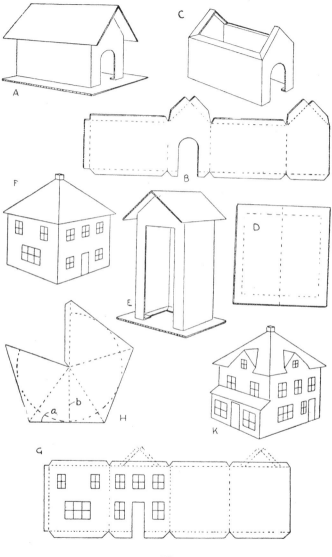

A

C

F

B

D

E

H

K

G

37

# KNITTING PROJECTS

From a pleasant and, to many, a soothing occupation for leisure hours, knitting has become a work of national importance. Through the *Daily Mail*, Lady Reading has issued an appeal for all the children who have been evacuated and for their mothers. A great number are from poor homes, and are unprepared for cold weather. They will need warm jerseys, socks and underclothes which they may not be able to afford to buy.

Needed most of all for the children are jerseys with collars, socks and stockings, gaiters, suits, skirts and vests. For mothers there are cardigans, jumpers, vests, bedjackets, etc. For babies, coatees, vests, shawls and cot blankets; and for the hospitals: bed-jackets, bed-socks, etc. Send the finished articles to the *Daily Mail* (Knitting Appeal), Northcliffe House, London, E.C.4.

Knitted articles will be in demand by members of all the fighting forces; sailors will need gloves from 11 to 11½ in. long, width 4½ in., finger length about 3½ in., and length of ribbing at wrist 3½ in. Mittens, which should be half finger length, and wristlets made in blue soft wool loosely knitted in 2-2 ribbing, 5 in. long and 3 in. wide. Blue wool pullovers, with or without three-quarter length sleeves, chest sizes from 34 to 40 in. and neck opening 6½ in. Seaboot stockings, length 26 in. to 28 in. made from a coarse, hard, natural wool. Circular knit blue wool scarves with a width of 9½ in. and a length of 48 in. Balaclava helmets in 3/3 ribbing with a length of 15 in. and a width of 7 in. in blue wool. These articles should be sent to The Secretary, Royal Naval War Comforts Committee, Admiralty, S.W.1.

Soldiers and airmen will need pullovers, helmets, gloves, socks and mittens, mufflers. Knitted goods for soldiers should be sent to the Officer i/c Army Comforts, 12, St. Mary's Butts, Reading, Berks., and for the Air Force to the Officer i/c R.A.F. Comforts.

The examples shown on Plates XVII and XXV are

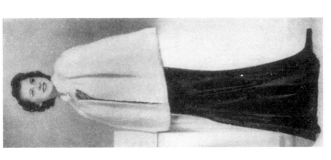

LADY'S CAPE MADE IN ASTRAKHAN WOOL.

LADY'S BRAIDED EVENING COATS IN CLOVER BOUCHÉ.

LADY'S CHECK COAT IN CLOVER BOUCHÉ.

PLATE XVI

CHILD'S COAT, PULL-UPS AND HOOD MADE IN TARGET 4-PLY WOOL.

COAT AND HAT FOR GIRL OF THREE YEARS MADE IN ASTRAKHAN WOOL.

SCHOOL GIRL'S THREE-PIECE MADE IN TARGET 3- AND 4-PLY WOOL.

taken from Constructive Knitting (Dryad Press, 2s. 6d.). This book also contains many suggestions for simple articles suitable for young fingers.

Women's sections in the newspapers, the weekly and monthly magazines devoted to dress and household duties, contain suggestions, but, in addition, special leaflets, containing detailed instructions, are published by the manufacturers of knitting wools and are obtainable in all wool shops. The illustrations on Plates XV and XVI, reproduced from designs by George Lee and Sons, Ltd., are a few of the original designs published by this firm. The check coat on Plate XV is particularly attractive and is made from Lee's Clover Bouche. The white cape on Plate XV made in Astrakhan wool is ideal wear for the black-out. The two evening coats, also made in Clover Bouche, with braided ornamentation, shown on Plate XV, are quite exclusive designs. For the children, the schoolgirls three-piece suit, shown on Plate XVI, is made with Target 3- and 4-ply wool. The little girl's coat and hat illustrated on Plate XVI is another example of the use of Lee's Astrakhan wool. The child's coat, pull-ups and hood made in Target 4-ply wool are especially attractive.

Special care should be taken with all knitting intended for use by members of the forces. It is essential that the wool should be of the finest quality, and with this object in view, socks, gloves and mittens for men should be knitted with Beehive or Cycle, Double Knitting or Paton's Super Wheeling. For service scarves, gloves, and stockings, use Paton's Rose or White Heather Fingering 4-ply. Details of the man's service pull-over, socks, gloves and mittens, shown on Plate XVII, will be found in Paton and Baldwin's leaflets Nos. 2758 and 2751. Instructions for the Woman's service cardigan and the scarf, gloves and stockings, shown on Plate XVII, are in Nos. 2760 and 2766.

# WOOL WINDER

The wool winder shown on page 41 is simple in construction and adjustable for various sizes in skeins. The base can be weighted to stand on a table, or a small G cramp can be used to keep it in place.

The arms are made with two lengths of 1¼ in. by ½ in. hardwood joined in the centre with a cross halving or lapped joint as shown in a separate detail. Prepare the two lengths to just over 13 in., and pare the ends to the correct length, the corners being pared down as shown. Mark off the centre, set out ¼ in. each side, and saw and pare out the grooves, one on one side and the other from the opposite side.

Draw a line along the top edges exactly in the middle, and then set out marks ½ in. apart, beginning ½ in. from the ends. Now provide four 5 in. lengths of iron or steel rod, having a diameter of approximately ⅛ in. Find a drill of the same size and then bore upright holes from each of the marks to a depth of 1 in., care being taken to keep them upright.

Fit the two lengths together, and then provide a 3 in. length of ¼ in. diameter iron rod, failing the metal rod, a length of beech dowelling will do. Bore a hole through the middle of the joint to take the rod, and then prepare a 3 in. square piece of plywood for a cap, and screw it on as shown. The base is made from a 6 in. by 6 in. square of 1 in. thick wood, bore a hole in the centre to a depth of ¾ in. to take the centre rod and then fit the arms in position. To give additional weight to the base, a square piece of lead sheet may be screwed on and covered with a piece of baize, flannel or felt which should be glued on. Easy running is assured if the holes are true and the rod covered with a little blacklead.

PLATE XVII

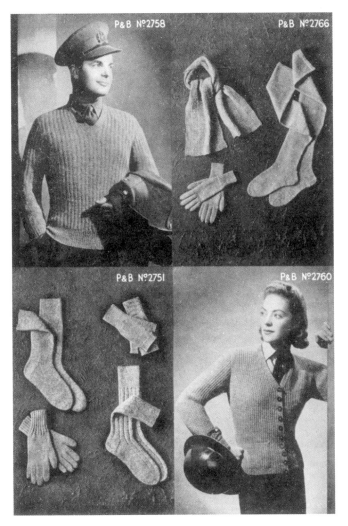

SERVICE PULLOVER, SOCKS, GLOVES, MADE OF BEE-
HIVE OR CYCLE, DOUBLE KNITTING (OR PATON'S
SUPER WHEELING, 3-PLY).

PLATE XVIII

SERVICE HELMETS, DESIGNS FROM PATON'S AND
BALDWIN'S LEAFLETS.

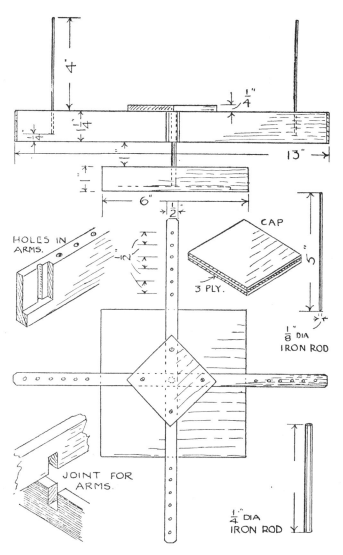

Labels within figure:
4'

1/4"

1/4"

1 1/4"

13"

6"

1/2"

HOLES IN ARMS.

2"

CAP

3 PLY.

5"

1/8" DIA IRON ROD

JOINT FOR ARMS.

1/4" DIA IRON ROD

CONSTRUCTION OF WOOL WINDER.

# PATCHWORK

Patchwork provides an excellent and economical way of putting to practical use all kinds of odds and ends of plain and coloured fabrics. Counterpanes, cushion covers, table cloths and innumerable small articles, by the exercise of patience and a little ingenuity, can be made highly decorative. Harmonising of colours and the matching of patterns will help in forming treatments that will transform otherwise unused or useless scraps into original designs.

The simplest patchwork is formed by squares of material sewn together and finished with a plain border. The chequer pattern shown at A on the next page, is quite effective when carried out in two colours, with the same colours used in the border. The size of the squares will, of course, depend on the material available and also the size of the finished work. For example a counterpane may have squares up to 6 in., but those on a cushion cover should not be more than 3 in. When a colour scheme has been evolved, the size of the square should be cut out in cardboard with allowance of a definite amount for turning in, and the material should be cut accurately to the template. In sewing up the squares it will be found simpler to sew the squares to form complete strips and then sew the strips together. Quilting will often help in finishing, as shown at B.

The above method applies to many other shapes, but it is not always possible to make up strips. The diamond patterns shown at C and D are effective for contrasting colours, suggestions for treatment can be found in stained glass windows. It is advisable at first to keep to geometrical patterns, there is so much variety to be obtained by suitable arrangements of simple shapes, that the more difficult round shapes need not be attempted.

Multi-coloured patchwork, like mosaic work, calls for careful scheming if it is to look attractive, but three colours can be worked into simple geometrical patterns

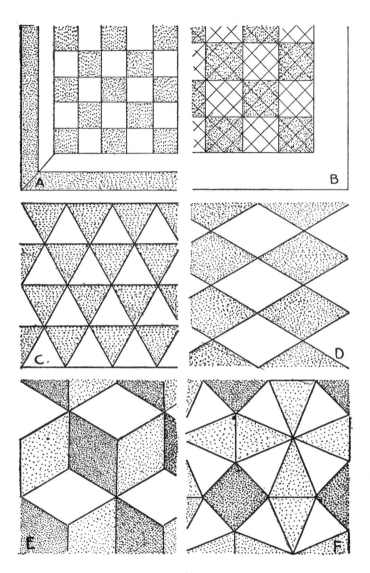

as indicated at E and F. The pattern at E is more suitable for three tones of the same colour, but in the pattern at F, three or four harmonising or contrasting colours can be used. It should be noted that special care should be taken to use pieces of approximately the same substance throughout; it is a mistake to mix thick and thin fabrics together in the same piece of patchwork.

The possibilities of using up scraps of leather in making pouffes, cushions, book covers, tea-cosies, etc., should not be overlooked in dealing with patchwork. It is often possible to purchase quite cheaply useful cuttings of thin leather, and with care they can be worked into useful and durable articles.

Patchwork is closely allied to appliqué and the combination of the two kinds of craftwork can be effectively arranged. A pattern which may be adapted to a large counterpane or a small cushion cover is shown at the top of the next page. The appliqué, shaded on the diagram, is suitable equally for a patchwork of squares, as at A, or a diamond pattern, as at B. Some care should be exercised in the selection of colours for both the groundwork as well as the applied pattern. The possibilities offer considerable scope to the artistic worker.

The patterns shown on page 47, and intended for appliqué, may be adapted for use in conjunction with patchwork; many other arrangements of similar or of purely geometrical forms will, no doubt, suggest themselves to the interested needlewoman. Border patterns can be designed in unlimited variety, and may be composed of simple shapes, as indicated at C and D, or with round forms, as at E and F. In the latter case considerable care will be needed in cutting out the shapes, which should be done with templates; much of the effect of a good design will be lost if the shapes are carelessly cut or proportioned.

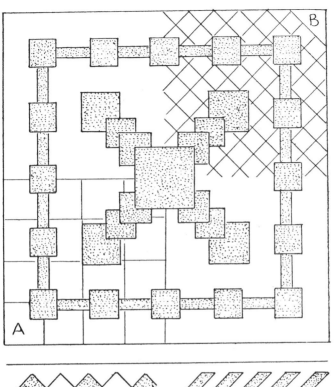

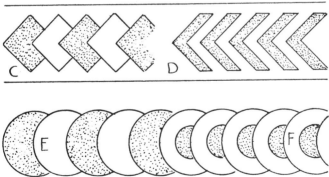

# APPLIQUÉ

Appliqué is a particularly simple yet most effective form of decoration, it can be carried out in various materials, but usually it is associated with needlework. One of the most attractive forms of appliqué is that of lace on satin and other materials ; for example a square, a single motif or a combination of motifs cut from lace, can be arranged suitably on a contrasting background, and either plainly stitched or buttonholed. Actually the same idea can be followed with other materials, one effective method is to apply lace to the vellum surface of a lamp shade, another is to apply black lace to the surface of a glass jam-jar and finish with a transparent varnish.

The motifs for appliqué may be single ones in the form of leaves or flowers, the design shown at the top of page 47 shows a simple leaf shape and the same leaf folded. The modern floral motif in the centre of the page is a combination of leaf and flower forms, it can be built up in the form of patchwork, simply embroidered, and then attached with the buttonhole stitch.

An ultra modern design is given at the bottom of the page ; this will be found most effective and offers a good opportunity for the use of colour. Cut-out patterns in figured cretonne or tapestry can be used with effect, borders can be worked on curtains and decoration provided for cushion covers. If it has been necessary to use black or dark grey materials for black-out curtains, the effect need not be gloomy ; it is not a difficult matter to cut out patterns in brilliant colourings and transform the drabbest material into a fabric of some beauty. Felt is an excellent material for use with appliqué methods, it is obtainable in a large range of colours and may be bound with a blanket stitch in wool.

Correct methods of cutting felt are shown on Plate XX, and examples of simple applique are shown on Plate XXI.

PLATE XIX

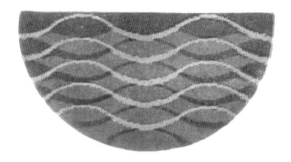

RUG DESIGNS.

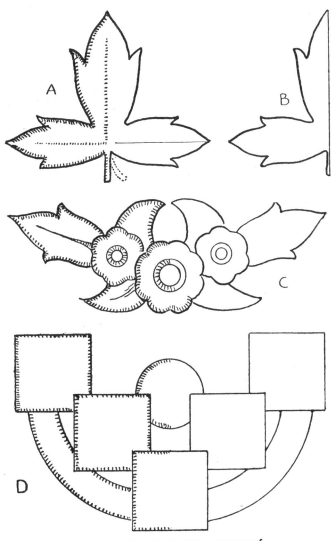

A

B

C

D

DESIGNS SUITABLE FOR APPLIQUÉ.

47

# LEATHER WORK

Of the many simple crafts suitable for the long evenings, leather work is one of the most practical. The outfit is neither extensive nor expensive, and need not be more than a saddler's punch or the more convenient punch-pliers shown on Plate XXII, a combined modeller and tracer, and two or three pattern stamps. In addition, provide scissors, a sharp knife, ruler and pencil. To begin with the material should be plain skiver which is used for lining and modelling calf for general work, and Persian calf used for gussets, pockets, partitions, etc. Thongs, resembling thin leather laces, are obtainable in various widths, $\frac{1}{16}$in. and $\frac{1}{8}$in. being most serviceable. Special stains are available for use when required.

A suitable piece of work to begin with is shown on page 49 in the form of a durable case for a gas mask. Made in calf, it consists of five pieces of leather which may, if desired, be lined with skiver. Cut the calf to the sizes given in the diagram, either tracing direct on to the leather or by first cutting templates from stiff paper. If skiver is used for a lining, it should be cut slightly larger than the required shape and pasted on the inside of the skin; rub out surplus paste from the centre outwards over a piece of paper placed on top.

The position of the thonging holes should be indicated by lines $\frac{1}{8}$ in. from the outside edges and by marks on the line $\frac{1}{4}$ in. apart. It is understood that the edges are all left true and even. Beginning at the bottom of the two pieces A and B, the lacing is carried up one side, around the top and down on the other. If the front portion is lined, it would be advisable to thong it across. The circular bottom piece is now laced up to complete the case, the end of the lace should be threaded under convenient loops. The strap is in two lengths joined together with a strip of skiver pasted on and then completely thonged on both sides. Secure the ends of

48

PLATE XX

CUTTING FELT FOR APPLIQUÉ.

PLATE XXI

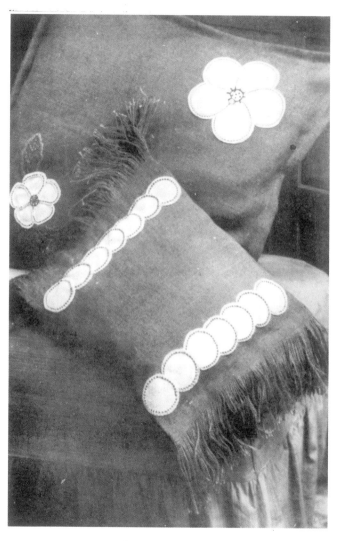

APPLIQUÉ WITH SIMPLE SHAPES.

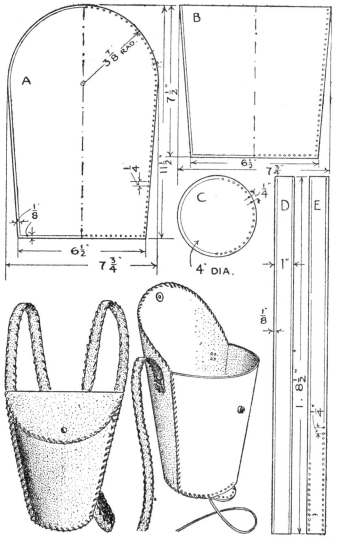

A

$3\frac{7}{8}$" RAD.

B

$7\frac{1}{2}$"

$11\frac{1}{2}$"

$\frac{1}{4}$"

$6\frac{1}{2}$"

$\frac{1}{8}$"

$6\frac{1}{2}$"

$7\frac{3}{4}$"

$7\frac{3}{4}$"

C

$\frac{1}{4}$"

4" DIA.

D   E

1"

$\frac{1}{8}$"

1.  $8\frac{1}{2}$"

$\frac{1}{4}$"

OBJECTS IN LEATHER WORK.

the strap to the back of the case with lacing; the flap should be secured with a large press stud.

A number of suggestions for useful bags are shown on page 51. One is a very easily made pouchette, illustrated in the centre at A, and the various parts are shown below at A, B, C and D. Suitable dimensions should be chosen, the parts cut out and marked for thonging, a suitable pattern for a stamp is shown at E. The thonging holes can be made with a saddler's punch, as indicated at F, using a piece of linoleum as a pad. The gusset is thonged as shown at G, and the work nearly completed at H.

A shopping bag or book carrier is illustrated at K, the top edges should be thinned and glued down before thonging, as indicated at L. The thonged handles are laced as shown. A more ambitious piece of work is shown at M. The construction is similar to that of the pouchette at A, but the work should be lined with skiver. The embossed pattern shown on the front flap of the bag should not be attempted without previous experience with the tracer and modelling tool. The leather cover of a writing case, as illustrated on Plate XXIV, is not a difficult pattern to begin with. The indentations are made with the tracer on the damped surface of the skin, but the pattern is drawn first on paper and then traced on the leather. The tracing point is drawn along the lines and will give a sufficient impress to allow of a deeper impression being made after the tracing paper is taken off. The leather must be sufficiently moist to allow the tracer to press well into the leather if the pattern is to be permanent. Patterns similar to that shown at M must be modelled from underneath as well as from the top. The detail at N indicates the colouring to be applied with stains. Fuller information about leather work, including some of the examples on the next page, will be found in " 101 Things for Girls to Do."

PLATE XXII

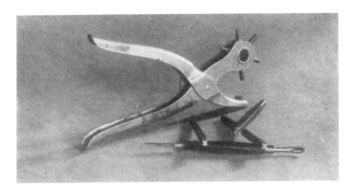

THE TOOLS USED IN LEATHER WORK.

A DECORATED LEATHER BAG BY J. H. PECKHAM.

PLATE XXIII

HOW TO USE PUNCH PLIERS.

USING THE MODELLER FOR DECORATION.

PLATE XXIV

A WRITING CASE COVER BY J. M. PECKHAM.

METHODS OF THONGING ON A WALLET

PLATE XXV

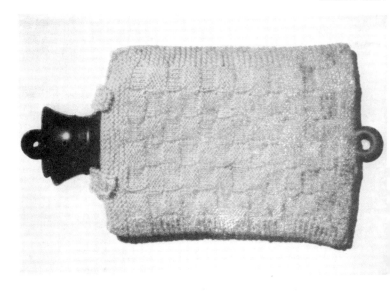

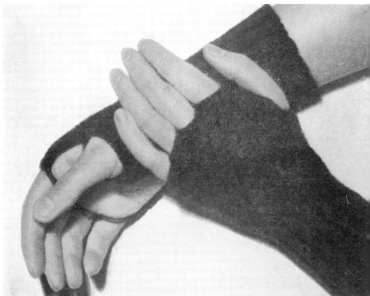

KNITTED COVER FOR HOT-WATER BOTTLE AND MITTENS, FROM "CONSTRUCTIVE KNITTING" (*Dryad Press*).

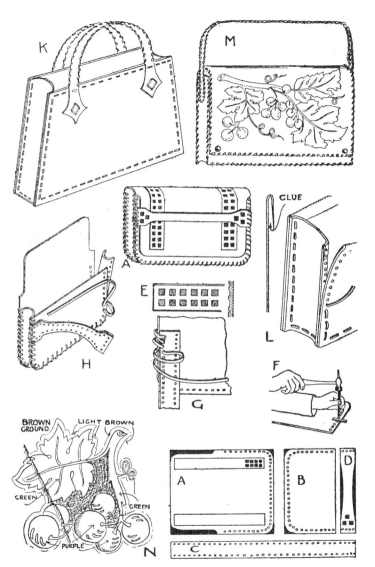

BAGS IN LEATHER WORK.

51

# USING UP SCRAPS OF METAL AND WOOD

There are many useful little articles which can be made from otherwise useless scraps of metal and odd pieces of wood. With the exercise of some ingenuity and ordinary care, many waste materials can be put to good use either as articles for home use or as acceptable presents.

The match-box rack, shown at 1 on the next page, is generally welcomed by the housewife, the match-box is rested on a ledge and held in position by a metal band. Variations can be made in the top of the wooden back, as indicated at 1A, 1B and 1C. The strip of metal may be decorated in several ways, a simple pattern being shown at 1D.

Strip brass can be made into a spring for use as a paper clip, as shown at 2. The piece of wood may be plain or decorated by simple knife cuts as indicated. The strip of brass should be bent to the required shape and hammered hard, using the head of another hammer or the surface of a flat iron as an anvil, as indicated at 2A.

Another particularly useful method of using up small scraps of metal is to form them into corner clips for a blotting pad. In this case the bottom of the pad should be cut from plywood to the required size of the blotting paper, preferably to the full size of a sheet approximately $15\frac{1}{2}$ in. by 11 in. The metal may be ordinary tinned sheet, brass, copper or pewter; the latter materials can be left polished, but it will be necessary to give the tin a coat or two of paint or enamel.

The shape of one of the corner pieces is shown at 3A, the amount bent over should allow for the thickness of the plywood and a few sheets of blotting paper. The method of marking out the metal is shown at 3B, the dotted lines show the position of the bends. An alternative to the decoration at 3 is shown at 3C. If it is necessary to purchase metal for the corner pieces, pewter will be found easier to work.

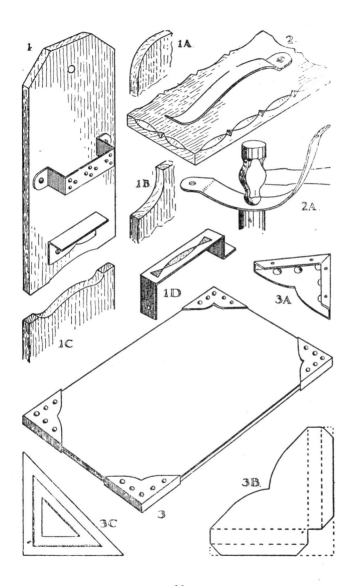

1
1A
2
1B
2A
1D
3A
1C
3A
3
3B
3C

# RUG MAKING

Turkey rug wool can be bought in over 100 different colours, and stencilled canvasses in colour, together with the exact amounts of wool can be obtained in a variety of patterns and shapes.

The principal stages in forming the knots for pile rug are shown on Plates XXVIII and XXIX. The wool is prepared by winding it round a gauge and cutting it into strands of uniform length with a sharp knife or a pair of scissors. The strands are first pulled through under the canvas mesh, the hook is pushed through the loop to catch the double strand, which is then pulled through the loop to form a knot and tightened up. All the knots are made in the same way.

To begin, turn back about 2 in. of canvas at the starting edge. Work the wool through this double thickness and finish off in the same way. In working oval, circular and semi-circular rugs, the surplus canvas is cut off, leaving a margin which is turned under and bound.

The best way to work is to sit at a table with the end of the work facing you. Work from left to right and let the completed fabric come forward. Place a weight on the canvas to resist the pull of the knot making. Do not be tempted to work out the pattern first, but carry on steadily from left to right, and always work in the same direction. If two people work at the rug together, they should sit side by side and not at opposite ends. When the last knot is finished, the completed fabric should be rubbed with the hands in one direction to remove loose fibres and freshen the pile, clip off any loose ends with scissors, and shake. Ends worked through double canvas can be overcast or left plain, the selvedges should be bound by holding the rug wrong side in front and work from left to right into the first row of holes. Insert a threaded needle into the first hole and bring it towards you, leaving about 3 in. to be

PLATE XXVI

DESIGNS FOR PILE RUGS MADE IN TURKEY WOOL.

PLATE XXVII

DESIGNS FOR PILE RUGS MADE IN TURKEY WOOL.

PLATE XXVIII

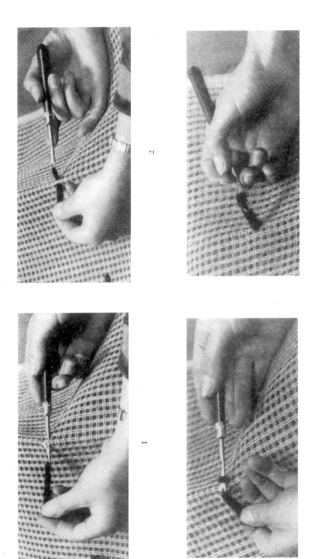

FOUR STAGES IN MAKING A PILE RUG WITH TURKEY WOOL, USING A HOOK.

PLATE XXIX

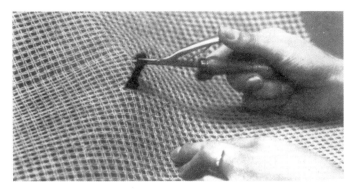

THREE STAGES IN MAKING A PILE RUG WITH TURKEY
WOOL, USING SPRING NIPPERS.

darned in later. Work forwards from the 1st hole to the 4th, then the 2nd to the 5th, and so on. In the case of curved edges, leave 2 in., turn under and sew binding to the outside edge of the rug with strong carpet thread and press the binding flat to the back of the rug.

The stages in making a short-pile rug are shown on Plate XXXII. The principle is to make a series of even loops knotted to the canvas, using a continuous length of wool. A short-pile needle for every colour, a gauge and scissors will be needed. Work similarly as described for long-pile rugs except that the row to be worked should lie along the edge of the table. First thread a needle with a length of wool, begin on the first row of the pattern and work from left to right of the double weft threads of the canvas. Insert the needle between the double threads of the first mesh; draw wool through leaving a free end as long as the gauge is wide. Hold this firm end and insert needle just above the double threads, taking care that the loop of the wool lies to the right of the needle. Draw wool through and a knot is made. Lay the gauge on the canvas, the upper edge being just beneath the knot. Pass wool under and over gauge; then insert needle between double threads of the next mesh so that the loop of the wool lies left of the needle. Draw wool snugly around gauge, insert needle just above the double threads of the same mesh with the wool lying to the right of the needle. Draw wool through once more to complete second stitch. Repeat along the row, working in colours as required and before the gauge is moved along, cut loops evenly.

There are two more methods of making rugs, one is to use a weaving frame and the other is carried out on canvas with rug wool by means of the cross stitch. Suggestions for the latter will be found in " 101 Things for Girls to Do." Pile rugs can also be made with strips of felt or cuttings from old silk stockings.

See Frontispiece and Plates XIX, XXX and XXXV for some clever designs and colour schemes.

# SOUPS

A stock pot is a necessity in every kitchen, as many kinds of scraps can be placed in it, all bones, pieces of gristle or trimmings which would otherwise be thrown away, and the liquor will make the base of soups or gravies, etc.

Reserve a large saucepan for the stock pot and boil it up each day. In the summer it should be turned out into a bowl after boiling, but in winter this is not necessary for it can be moved off the fire, leaving the lid partly open and allowing it to get cold.

In making the stock the bones, etc., should be put into cold water, breaking up all bones and cutting the meat into small pieces. Simmer gently for at least six hours; it can be left on the lowest possible gas jet all night, being sure the flame is free from draught and not likely to go out.

Allow quite a quart of water to each pound of meat, keeping the pot closely covered during simmering. The carcases of chicken or game or rabbit bones add a nice flavouring to stock, and all liquor in which meat has been boiled can be added with advantage, but it should be remembered, that salt should not be added to stock, as in evaporation the stock would be too salt and spoil the soup. Any necessary seasoning should be left until the soup is made.

In buying meat for the stock pot get the leanest and freshest possible, allowing it to stand in the water for a time before bringing it very slowly to the boil. When cold remove all fat from the surface; this should not be wasted but clarified and used for frying, etc.

This stock is suitable for making all kinds of soups, adding the desired flavourings needed. Packets in different flavourings can be purchased cheaply, they make good soups and are quite nutritious providing the stock in which they are mixed is of good quality. When using packet soup, enrichen it by adding a knob of butter.

Vegetables should not, as a rule, be put in the stock pot, as they are liable to turn the liquor sour. They can be used sparingly, but the flavour will overpower the meat, the vegetables should be whole or large pieces and only added after the stock has been boiled and thoroughly skimmed.

It is better to use vegetables as a base for an inexpensive vegetable soup, which can be made as follows : Take three carrots, or more if small, two good sized onions, a turnip, two tomatoes, a stick of celery, a head of lettuce a bouquet garni (parsley, thyme and bay leaf) a blade of mace, if liked, three ounces of butter, two quarts of water, and salt to taste.

Cut the onions, turnip and carrots into thin slices and the celery into small pieces. Melt the butter in a saucepan, put in the vegetables, and boil gently for half an hour, keeping the lid on and occasionally stirring to avoid burning.

Shread the lettuce, and when the vegetables are cooked, place all together in the saucepan with the water, bring to the boil slowly and simmer gently for one and a half hours. Skimming off the scum as it rises.

The soup either can be strained, or the vegetables pressed through a fine sieve to serve as a thickening. Baked snippets of bread can be served if desired.

If celery is unobtainable a teaspoonful of celery seeds, tied up in muslin, will answer the purpose for flavouring.

All dried pulse vegetables, such as peas, beans and lentils, make good soups, they are rich in protein, but contain no fat, this must be added when cooking. All the above vegetables (with the exception of Egyptian lentils) must be soaked for at least twelve hours, and should be cooked very slowly, salt added only just before being served.

# ECONOMICAL SAVOURY DISHES
## Using Up Cold Meat, Etc.

To make an ordinary suet pudding mixture, add half a pound of stewing steak, which should be wiped dry, cut into dice, dropped into the mixture and separated to keep it apart as much as possible. Pepper and salt to taste. A small chopped onion added, if desired, is an improvement. Boil for three hours. Serve with a good thick gravy.

The above makes a good stand-by for a cold day, and one that children love.

MOCK DUCK. Take half a pound of sausage meat, quarter of a pound of breadcrumbs, two small onions lightly cooked and chopped, a little sage, pepper and salt. Mix all together, place in a pie dish, and bake until nicely browned. Serve with apple sauce.

BACON PUDDING. Roll out a suet crust as for roly poly pudding, add four or five rashers of bacon, removing rind; sprinkle a little dried sage and a small onion chopped fine on the bacon, tie up in a cloth and boil for three hours.

SHEPHERD'S PIE. Everyone knows shepherd's pie, made with cold minced meat, onion, etc., but the secret of the success of this dish is to be sure and let the gravy (which should be a rich, thick one) get quite cold before adding it to the meat.

RISSOLES. If potatoes have to be cooked, especially to mix with the ingredients for rissoles, etc., slice and cook a couple of onions with them, this imparts a delicious flavour and saves the time taken to fry onions separately.

A pleasant change is made by peeling several large potatoes, cutting them in half lengthwise scoop out a hollow in the middle, bake them in the oven as for baked potatoes. When finished, fill the hole with a tasty mince, sprinkle a few bread crumbs on top and put back in the oven to heat thoroughly.

MEAT PATTIES. For a change use up cold meat (or fresh minced beef can be used) by making it into meat patties. Make a thick mince nicely seasoned, line patty tins with a meat pastry, add a little of the mince and cover with pastry, not forgetting to prick the top with a fork. This will prove an economical dish as a very little mince goes a long way.

CORNISH PASTIES. These are generally accept-able. Make a meat pastry with 3 oz. of fat to $\frac{1}{2}$ lb. of flour, 1 teaspoonful of baking powder, 1 eggspoonful of salt. For the filling take $\frac{1}{4}$ lb. of beef, $\frac{1}{4}$ lb. of potatoes, partly cooked, dessertspoonful of finely chopped onion, 2 tablespoonfuls of nice gravy, sprinkling of mixed herbs, salt and pepper to taste. Cut the meat and potatoes into dice and mix all together with the gravy. Rub the fat lightly into the flour, baking powder, and salt, and mix it with a little water (it must not be too moist). Divide the paste into eight equal portions keeping them as round as possible. Pile an eighth of the mixture into the centre of each piece, wet the edges all round and join together on the top to form a frill. Prick them here and there with a fork, and bake in a moderate oven for about half an hour.

CORNED BEEF, so much cheaper than fresh meat, can be used in innumerable ways, and with it many tasty and inexpensive dishes can be made. Below are a few recipes.

RISSOLES made with corned beef instead of any cold meat scraps are delicious either hot or cold. An onion should be cooked with the potatoes as suggested previously. Seasoning with herbs and fry in boiling fat to a nice golden brown.

Another recipe for corned beef is to make a pie with potatoes, a little chutney and tomatoes. Grease a pie dish and place $\frac{1}{2}$ lb. of sliced tomatoes in the bottom. Cut 1 lb. of corned beef into dice, moisten with a little good, cold gravy, add pepper and salt to taste, place this on the top of the tomatoes and sprinkle a generous helping of chutney or Pan Yan pickle on top. Cover with mashed potatoes, with knobs of dripping or margarine dotted on top. Cook in a fairly hot oven for about $\frac{1}{2}$ an hour.

Another tasty dish, using corned beef, is to bake several large potatoes in their skins, allowing one potato for two people.

Make a mixture of corned beef (a 1 lb. tin will make a lot), season with onion (parboiled) and pepper and salt to taste, and add a little butter or margarine. When the potato is thoroughly cooked, cut in half, scoop out the contents, mix with the mixture, put back in the skins, rubbing it with a fork into a little mound, place small knobs of butter or margarine on top, and put back into the oven to thoroughly heat through.

Readers are advised to listen to the broadcast talks by Miss Ann Hardy. Here are a few typical examples of the help she is giving.

BOILED RABBIT. Take a rabbit, 1 carrot, 1 onion, a little celery, 1 clove, $\frac{1}{4}$ lb. of rice, 3 pints of hot stock or water, pepper and salt to taste. Clean and wash rabbit, leave to soak in tepid water for one hour. Cut vegetables into dice, stick clove into onion, wash rice, remove liver, etc., from the rabbit, put it into stock, bring to the boil, skim well, then add the rice and vegetables, simmer gently for $1\frac{1}{2}$ hours. Serve with onion sauce.

If joints are difficult to obtain, a sheep or lamb's heart stuffed and brazed, served with a good gravy, will be found inexpensive, and makes a nice meal.

Liver also is good ; its food value is very high. If it seems hard, fry gently on both sides, and stew it. Or if minced with an onion and served on rice it makes a nice change.

OX KIDNEY makes a nice supper dish. It should be gently stewed and, when cold, cut up and put through the mincer. Add the mince to the stock, and heat it slowly, thicken well and serve hot on pieces of toast.

# MEATLESS DISHES

A CHEESE DISH. Take 3 oz. of grated cheese, 1 egg beaten, season to taste, not forgetting mustard, add 2 tablespoonfuls of milk, mix all together and allow to stand for an hour. Place in buttered dish and cook from 20 minutes to half an hour in medium oven.

AN EGG DISH. Take 1 small tin of tomatoes, 1 small onion minced, 1 oz. of margarine, 4 eggs. Fry onion in the margarine until slightly brown, add the tomato and simmer for a few minutes. Divide it into four ramekins or similar dishes. Break an egg into each dish, bake in oven until set; when dishing up add a little tomato sauce. Garnish with Paprika.

SAVOURY RICE. Take $\frac{1}{4}$ lb. of rice, 1 onion, 2 oz. of margarine, 3 oz. of grated cheese, pepper and salt. Wash the rice, place into about 1 pint of boiling water, put onion in whole, cook gently until rice and stock and water is absorbed. If rice is not quite done a little more water should be added. Finally remove the onion, add margarine and season, mix in half the cheese, place in greased pie dish, put rest of cheese on top and bake in oven until cheese melts.

CHEESE BALLS. Take 2 oz. of grated cheddar cheese, 1 oz. of flour, 1 egg, salt, pepper and cayenne. Mix the cheese, flour and yoke of egg together, add salt, pepper and cayenne to taste. Then whip the white of egg to a stiff froth and stir it gently into the rest of the ingredients. Drop the mixture in large teaspoonfuls in deep boiling fat and fry until nicely browned.

CURRIED RICE. Take 4 oz. of rice, 2 oz. of butter or margarine, 1 tomato, 2 shallots chopped fine, 1 teaspoonful of curry powder, 1 tablespoonful of cream, 1 hard-boiled egg, 1 gill of stock, 1 gill of brown sauce, salt, pepper, mace, and nutmeg.

Wash the rice, thoroughly drain, and dry. Fry the shallots slightly in hot margarine, gradually sprinkle in the curry powder, cook for a few minutes, then add the rice and cook, shaking well over the fire. Add the tomato (skinned and cut into dice) and the stock, some cream and sauce, season to taste with pepper, salt, mace and nutmeg. Cook slowly until the rice is tender, adding more stock to prevent the rice becoming too dry. When finished pile it upon a dish garnished with slices of hard boiled egg. If cream should be too expensive, skim a tablespoonful off the top of the milk.

A variant of the ordinary macaroni cheese is made with 6 oz. of macaroni, 3 oz. of grated cheese, $1\frac{1}{2}$ oz. of butter or margarine, 1 oz. of flour, $\frac{3}{4}$ pint of milk, $\frac{1}{2}$ teaspoonful of made mustard and some brown bread crumbs, salt and pepper to taste.

Break up the macaroni into small pieces, place in slightly salted boiling water, boil until tender, and drain well. Melt the butter or margarine, stir in flour, add milk, and boil well stirring all the time. Add the macaroni cheese, mustard, salt and pepper, and mix all together thoroughly. Place in greased pie dish and sprinkle brown bread and grated cheese on top, adding knobs of butter here and there and bake in quick oven until nicely browned.

Another way is to boil $\frac{1}{2}$ lb. of macaroni in milk until tender, mix in 6 oz. of grated cheese, beat 1 egg and pour over, put small knobs of butter or margarine in small pieces over the top. Bake in oven until nicely browned.

A less known way to use up cold cauliflower is to break it up into small pieces, dip in batter and fry in boiling fat. Drain well and sprinkle with grated cheese.

Another easy dish made with cauliflower is to use either one freshly boiled or any cold left-over. Make a nicely seasoned onion sauce, pour over the cauliflower, sprinkle with brown bread crumbs, adding a few knobs of butter or margarine on top. Bake in hot oven for about 20 minutes, until nicely browned.

Pancakes are very nice with grated cheese added. Try them for a change, they will be found delicious served with spinach.

EGGS AND TOMATOES. A nice supper dish which can be prepared during the day and served cold. Allow a good sized tomato for each person, which should be firm and not too ripe. Cut the top of the tomato to form a lid, scoop out some of the inside and season with pepper and salt. Break an egg carefully into each tomato, put on the lids and bake in a moderately warm oven until the eggs are set. Serve cold with salad.

Another tasty supper dish and quite inexpensive is made with a tin of Heinz beans and grated cheese. Heat the beans and place on buttered toast, sprinkle generously with grated cheese; place under the grill and brown lightly.

Another quickly prepared supper dish is made with water biscuits and cheese. Allow two for each person. Butter them and sprinkle lightly with grated cheese and a little pepper, unless the cheese is strong. Place in a moderate oven until the cheese melts, then serve as quickly as possible.

Use up cold potatoes and cabbage; made into cakes, they make a nice addition to a meal. Mash both smoothly together, season with pepper and salt, a little onion parboiled. Moisten with some white sauce, mix a beaten egg to bind together. Form into round cakes, flour, and fry a nice brown in boiling fat.

TOMATO PIE. Take a good-sized onion, slice very thinly and fry until nicely browned. Take 1 lb. of tomatoes, skin and cut into slices. Grease a pie dish, put a layer of onion at the bottom then a layer of tomatoes, seasoning well. Follow with a layer of breadcrumbs with knobs of butter or margarine dotted over, then a second layer and so on until the dish is nearly full. Add a layer of nicely mashed potatoes on top with a few more knobs of butter or margarine added. Cook until nicely browned.

# FISH DISHES

Fish to be perfectly fresh should be quite stiff, plump and firm, the eyes should be clear, and the gills red coloured. When the freshness has worn off the flesh becomes flabby, easily indented with the finger, and the eyes dull and glazed. This should be particularly noticed as it is dangerous to eat fish unless perfectly fresh.

Below are given a few inexpensive fish recipes.

HADDOCK AND TOMATOES :

Take 1½ lb. of fresh haddock fillets and ¾ lb. of tomatoes (or more if liked).

Place some small pieces of fish in the bottom of a casserole or, failing this, a covered pie dish. Add a layer of tomatoes cut fairly thin, pepper and salt to taste, a layer of fish again, and then tomatoes to make three layers. Finally add knobs of butter, or margarine, about an ounce, bake in a slow oven until cooked. Serve with plain white sauce, made with some of the liquor out of the casserole, to which, if desired, may be added a little French or plain mustard.

Hake may be used instead of haddock for this dish, it has a more delicate flavour, but is more expensive.

A still cheaper fish is herrings ; they are usually split and grilled or fried, or they can be soused, that is, cooked in a covered dish with a few cloves and one bay leaf, and vinegar and water just to cover them.

Serve hot or cold.

STUFFED HERRINGS :

Another tasty way of cooking herrings is to split and bone them, cut in half and roll them up with veal stuffing in the middle, and cook with vinegar, etc., as above, but without the bay leaf.

Stuffed with finely sliced onion instead of the veal stuffing makes a nice change.

MACKEREL is considered the most digestible fish.

Soused mackerel is also delicious when cooked

similarly to herrings with vinegar and water, with or without a bay leaf and cloves.

Mackerel may be cooked under the grill and served with mustard sauce, or steamed and served with parsley sauce, to make a satisfying meal.

Turbot and halibut both yield a large proportion of proteid, but are more expensive to buy.

Steam instead of boil your fish.

Boiled fish loses some of its nutritive value, it is always advisable to steam it in order to retain the nutrients. The result is certainly more tasty than when it is boiled.

It is generally more economical to purchase more fish than is actually needed for the meal, as cold fish can be used to make many tasty dishes. FISH PIE is very simply and quickly made. Break up remains of fish left, remove all bones and place in the bottom of a pie dish. Boil two eggs hard, then chop up to make a fairly thick egg sauce, seasoned to taste. Pour over the fish and mix thoroughly, place some mashed potatoes on top with a few knobs of butter or margarine, cook in oven until the top is nicely browned.

The pie can also be made with just a few slices of potatoes above the fish mixture, and finished off with a pie crust to make a change.

A similar dish to above is made by mixing the fish in the same way, but using equal quantities of breadcrumbs and fish, making the egg sauce and mixing it altogether, and steam in a pudding basin for an hour or longer, according to size. Serve with a sauce to which a few drops of anchovy essence has been added, or juice of lemon if preferred.

FISH CAKES. These are very economical, and any cold fish is suitable; bone the fish and mix with equal quantity of potatoes, add a little chopped parsley, a squeeze of lemon, and a little anchovy if liked. But it should be remembered in using anchovy essence that it is very salt, so little if any other salt should be used.

Mix all thoroughly together, then add an egg (or two) if there is a lot of the mixture to bind it. Then make into cakes and dip into flour or breadcrumbs, and fry in boiling fat until just nicely browned.

These will be found delicious served hot or cold.

Another form of fish cake is very nice made with tinned salmon, in the same way as above, using the salmon instead of cooked fish.

Fresh salmon is rather an expensive dish, but Empire salmon, which is much cheaper, can hardly be distinguished from the fresh if cooked carefully. Place the fish in a casserole or covered pie dish, with a little pepper and salt, and a lemon sliced very thinly placed on top with knobs of butter on top of the lemon. Cook slowly for three-quarters to one hour. Serve with white sauce, to which a little anchovy essence has been added, just sufficient to make it a pale pink. No salt.

Remove the lemon and pour sauce over the fish.

COD. Fillets of cod with streaky bacon make a nice change.

Place the fillets in a greased casserole or covered dish, season with a little pepper only, cover with rashers of streaky bacon (removing the rinds), put a second layer and cover again with bacon.

Cook from half to three-quarters of an hour, according to quantity. Uncover and give it a few minutes longer to get nicely browned.

Stew made of cod is another inexpensive dish.

Slice some onions and put in boiling salted water for ten minutes, drain thoroughly. Boil the fish for a few minutes with a little salt, long enough to be skinned easily. Skin and bone it, place in stew-pan in alternate layers with some onion, and thick slices of potatoes. Cover with hot water and simmer slowly until the potatoes are cooked. Serve with thick parsley sauce if liked.

CURRIED COD. Remove all bones from 1 lb. Melt 3 oz. of butter in a frying-pan, add one medium sized

PLATE XXX

RUG DESIGNS.

onion, brown in the butter. Nicely brown the fish. Put the butter and onion in a stew-pan. Thicken ½ pint of white stock with ½ oz. of flour, adding 1 oz. of butter, and put into the stew-pan. Add 1 teaspoonful of curry powder and let it all simmer for ten minutes. Add ¼ pint of milk, and salt and cayenne to taste.

Put in the fish, boil up and serve.

Any other fish can be curried in this way.

KEDGEREE. Boil 4 oz. of rice until tender, dry and let cool.

Take an equal quantity of any cold fish. Remove all bones and pieces of skin, and divide into flakes and put into a saucepan. Add the rice, together with 1½ oz. of butter (or margarine), salt and cayenne to taste.

Stir all ingredients over the fire until quite hot. Add two eggs lightly beaten. Stir in gently, serve when the eggs are set, it must on no account be allowed to boil.

Try a little grated cheese on grilled fish for a change.

SCALLOPED FISH. Use about ½ lb. to ¾ lb. of any cold fish, break it up after removing bones and skin.

Make a nice white sauce with butter or margarine, flour, and ½ pint of milk. When cooked add the fish, together with one teaspoonful of Anchovy essence, one teaspoonful of ketchup and a little made mustard, salt and pepper to taste. Stir over the fire until thoroughly heated throughout.

Now nearly fill scallop shells with the mixture, cover the top lightly with bread crumbs, place small pieces of butter or margarine on top and brown nicely in a hot oven. A little grated cheese mixed with the bread crumbs will give an added piquancy.

# BOTTLING FRUIT AND VEGETABLES

Bottling is the most economical method of preserving fruit when sugar is scarce. The fruit can be preserved whole or in pulp, simply and inexpensively, the bottles for the purpose are cheap and readily obtainable, those with screw tops being preferable. A large saucepan, a small galvanised bath or a large fish kettle will answer for a steriliser and, with the addition of a thermometer, the equipment is complete. New bottles should be examined for flaws, placed in cold water and slowly brought up to the boil to temper them and prevent breakage.

The best results are obtained with whole fruit when it is slightly under-ripe, if some of the fruit is ripe, it is better to separate one from the other and sterilise them independently. First wash all fruit, except raspberries and loganberries, etc., remove anything unsound and prepare it by removing the hulls from raspberries, the tops and tails of gooseberries, the stalks of currants and cherries, the stones of the latter, as well as plums, may be removed. Apples and pears should be peeled and quartered.

Pack the fruit in perfectly clean bottles, taking care not to bruise it, and then fill up the bottles to the brim. Allow them to stand for a few minutes for the water to settle and then pour in again to the brim. Screw the cap of the bottle not more than a turn or so, leaving space for air to escape. Place as many bottles as possible in the pan and fill up with cold water to within 1 in. of the top and then gradually bring up to the required heat, approximately 160 degrees. The bottles should be removed with the cap screwed down tightly and allowed to cool slowly. A special leaflet on fruit preservation is published by the Ministry of Agriculture and Fisheries.

In dealing with vegetables, they may be dried, bottled or placed in jars between layers of salt. The vegetables to be bottled should be clean, scalded or blanched by either boiling water or steam, by placing them in clean butter muslin before being dipped into the boiling water, or placed in the steamer for a few minutes. They are then plunged into cold water, removed at once, drained and packed into hot jars or bottles which are filled with boiling water, left for the required time and then removed and sealed.

Asparagus should be cut to suitable size, blanched for three minutes, placed tips upwards in bottle. Add salt to the boiling water, one teaspoonful to one quart and boil for one hour before sealing.

Beans should be graded for size and blanched for ten minutes. Add salt as above and boil one hour for each pint.

Beet should be selected small, the tops only trimmed, blanched for five minutes, plunged in cold water, and skinned. Add salt as above, and boil for three-quarters of an hour for pint size.

Brussels sprouts should be carefully selected and placed in salted water for one hour. Blanch for ten minutes and boil three-quarters of an hour for one pint.

Carrots should be small and quite clean, blanched for five minutes, dipped in cold water and skinned, add salt as above and boil as for beet. Celery should be trimmed and cut into short lengths, blanched for three minutes, add salt as above and boil for three-quarters of an hour for one pint. Leeks can be treated similarly, and onions, if not pickled, can be bottled in the same way as carrots.

Peas should be ripe and shelled, blanched for three minutes and boiled for one hour for one pint.

Vegetable salad can be bottled by preparing cubes of carrots, cauliflower, celery and slices of French beans, and onions together with peas. Place altogether, mix, blanch for five minutes and then boil for one hour per pint.

Runner beans will keep for a long time if placed in large jars between layers of salt. Select the beans carefully, prepare them as for ordinary cooking in uniform lengths, wash and drain thoroughly. Prepare the jars, they should be perfectly clean, and place a thin layer of common salt at the bottom. Now place a layer of beans about 1 in. or so, then sprinkle more salt and repeat with each layer of beans until the jar is full. Press down lightly and fill right up. The top of the jar should be covered with a cork or with greaseproof or parchment paper and left in a cool place until required. When needed for use, the beans should be taken out, washed thoroughly to remove the salt and then cooked in the ordinary way, no salt being required. The above method is excellent for utilising surplus beans, but care should be taken to select the beans before they become too old and stringy.

Many vegetables can be dried in an ordinary oven. Spinach, parsley and mint, peas and beans of all kinds, as well as carrots, parsnips, and turnips. Spinach, parsley and mint should be blanched, cooled in water and drained. Peas and beans should be blanched in water containing a little bi-carbonate of soda, cooled and drained. The roots should be skinned and sliced and steamed for a few minutes. Wire or wooden trays, lined with hessian, should be made to fit the oven ; the vegetables should be spread on the trays and placed in the oven which should not be hot, the temperature must not exceed 160 degrees. The best way of storing dried vegetables is to place them in paper bags and hang them in a dry cupboard or suspend them on the wall in the kitchen ; on no account should the contents of the bags be allowed to get damp. Whenever there is a surplus of the above vegetables and it is not convenient to bottle them all, drying is a useful method of preservation. It is possible to dry such fruit as apples, pears and plums, they should be ripe and sound. Peel and slice the apples and pears, the plums should be cut in half and stoned.

# PRESERVING EGGS IN WATERGLASS

Waterglass (a strong solution of silicate of soda) is by far the most convenient way of preserving eggs, especially when they are cheap, for use when they are scarce. New laid eggs may be kept quite fresh for at least six months; even after twelve months they are quite as nice as foreign eggs.

Special galvanised pails fitted with a wire basket may be obtained, and the concentrated waterglass is available in sealed tins. Considerable care must be taken to dilute the waterglass according to the instructions supplied with the tin, as the strength of the liquid varies. Anything from five to ten times the bulk of clean boiling water may be needed, and the utmost care must be taken to mix the waterglass with the water; thorough stirring is essential. Sufficient solution to cover the eggs must be provided.

There are two methods of using the waterglass solution, one, quite satisfactory for preserving for a few weeks, is to dip the eggs into the solution and dry them off; they can then be stored in the cool on shelves or trays. The most satisfactory method is to immerse the eggs entirely and keep them covered until they are required for use. Although not essential, it is as well to see that all the eggs are clean, any that are cracked should not be placed in the solution. If a wire basket is available, all the eggs to be preserved should be laid carefully, the pail should be filled to one-third with the solution and the basket lowered carefully and then, if necessary, filled to cover the top layer.

In dealing with a clean galvanised pail without a basket, place a layer of eggs in the bottom, cover with the solution, then place another layer, cover again and continue until the pail is full. It is always advisable to place the eggs in the preservative as soon as possible after they are laid.

# WATERLESS COOKING

There is a considerable water content to every food we eat—a pure water supplied by nature—quite sufficient for cooking purposes. In most cases, additional water does no more than dissolve a large proportion of valuable salts, and unless all the water added for cooking purposes is utilised for soup, much of the health-giving properties of the food are lost. Cabbages, for example, contain nearly 90 per cent. of water, carrots 85 per cent., potatoes 75 per cent., and meat nearly 50 per cent.

Foods cooked in their own natural juices can be cooked in very low temperatures, thus retaining the full flavour, the mineral and soluble salts and the content of valuable vitamins ; this ensures better digestion and, therefore, better health.

There are other advantages to be gained by using a waterless cooker, these are a saving in food, in fuel and in labour. The saving in food is caused by the fact that meat, for example, does not shrink, for loss in this direction may amount to 25 per cent. The saving in fuel is quite considerable, as the whole of a meal can be cooked in one utensil with a small gas ring at a saving of quite 50 per cent., even with the greatest care. Instead of several saucepans and baking dishes, there is only one container with two or more small fittings.

The illustrations on Plate XXXI show the several parts of the " Merton " British Waterless Cooker, obtainable in two sizes—medium (4 to 6 persons), and large (8 to 10 persons). It consists of a flat lid, A, a circular pan, B, from 2 in. to 2½ in. deep, suitable for steaming puddings, vegetables, fish and fruit. Two D-shaped pans as at C, both with two handles to facilitate easy removal ; they are suitable for any food to be steamed, or, by removing the handles, can be used as cake tins. A large tripod, D, is used to support the pans. The base, E, is a strong and deep steel tray which supports the cooker and distributes the heat.

PLATE XXXI

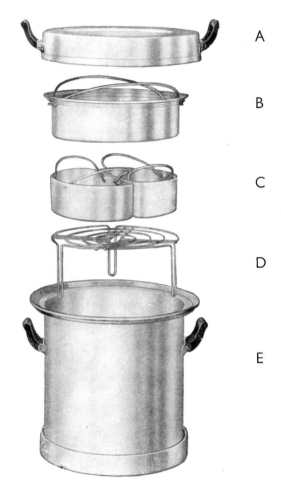

A

B

C

D

E

THE BRITISH WATERLESS COOKER,
SHOWING THE PARTS.

PLATE XXXII

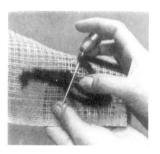

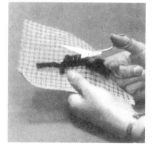

FIVE STAGES IN MAKING A SHORT PILE RUG WITH
TURKEY WOOL.

# EGG PRODUCTION

Half a dozen hens from good stock, properly housed and fed, will provide sufficient eggs for a small family. They should be pullets raised from pedigree stock and come, if possible, from a good egg-laying strain. There are many breeds to choose from, but it has been found that Rhode Island Reds give excellent results and provide excellent table poultry.

If the hens are to produce eggs in plenty, they must be well housed, well fed and given regular attention. As a rule quite half their food can be supplied from household scraps, the remainder should be grain. It will be necessary to register with a local corn merchant in order that a supply of suitable grain will be available.

As a rule the food should be distributed over the run and not confined to one spot. A good supply of clean water and occasional greenstuff should be supplied. Too much soft food should be avoided, but in very cold weather a small quantity of mash can be provided. It is advisable to cover the run with a couple of inches or so of clean gravel mixed with a small quantity of broken oyster shell and other grit. The gravel does not retain the wet like grass and provides the hens with plenty of exercise in finding the grain thrown over it.

When the hens become broody they should be supplied with a sitting of eggs, and it is well worth paying a good price for pedigree eggs. Separate nest boxes should be provided for each sitting hen, and it will be found quite profitable to rear the pullets for new layers and fatten the cockerels for the table. Laying hens should not be kept after two years, they are then suitable for boiling. For purposes of egg supply there is no need to keep a cockerel, it is much better to replenish the stock from sittings or from young pullets purchased from a reliable breeder.

# HAY-BOX COOKING

The hay-box is a simple device designed to save fuel. Soups, stews, porridge, puddings, etc., are first brought up to the boil, placed in the hay-box and left unattended for several hours. An earthenware stew-pan of porridge boiled up last thing at night, placed in the hay-box will be completely cooked and still hot at breakfast time.

The hay-box should be made as large as possible in relation to the size of the stew-pan. For a pan measuring 9 in. diameter, the box should be at least 18 in. each way. A suggestion is given on the next page for adapting a tea-chest. It is, however, quite a simple matter to make a convenient box with plywood stiffened by suitable framing.

To adapt a tea-chest, retain the lead foil lining and secure it with tacks along the top edge inside. Stiffen the lid with strips of $1\frac{1}{2}$ in. by $\frac{3}{4}$ in. wood, and hinge it to the box. Prepare a piece of plywood to fit inside the box, stiffen it with a frame of $1\frac{1}{2}$ in. by $\frac{3}{4}$ in. wood, as indicated, and then provide a piece of material to form a bag which should be deep enough when filled with straw to occupy one-third of the inside.

The hay-bag, which forms a cushion to rest on the top of the stew-pan, may be made of sacking, hessian, or any other suitable material, and filled with chopped hay. The lower portion of the box should be well packed with hay, and when the stew-pan is bedded in the hay there should be close contact with the cushion, as indicated in the section shown on the next page. In use, the pan containing the food is placed without loss of time into the box. Scoop out a recess for the pan inside the box, place the pan, without removing the lid, in the recess as soon as the contents have boiled, pack closely and then fit on the cushion. If a box is specially made, or a packing case adapted for the purpose, the inside should be lined with newspaper or brown paper.

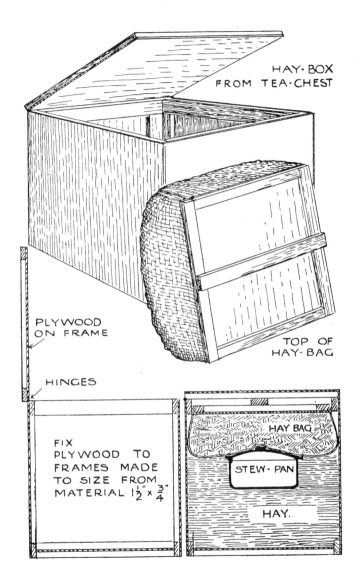

HAY·BOX
FROM TEA·CHEST

TOP OF
HAY·BAG

PLYWOOD
ON FRAME

HINGES

FIX
PLYWOOD TO
FRAMES MADE
TO SIZE FROM
MATERIAL $1\frac{1}{2}'' \times \frac{3}{4}''$

HAY BAG

STEW·PAN

HAY.

# EASILY MADE POULTRY HOUSE

A continual supply of eggs will make a welcome addition to a rationed food supply, but unless the fowls are properly housed, poultry keeping is apt to be disappointing. Laying hens must have adequate protection in bad weather and as large an area as possible for exercise.

A simple form of poultry house which is most easily and economically built is shown on the next page, it comprises two 8 ft. by 4 ft. sheets of either asbestos or beaver board, attached to a triangular framework of $1\frac{1}{2}$ in. by $1\frac{1}{2}$ in. wood filled in at both ends with weather or matchboarding. The asbestos sheet requires no further treatment, but beaver board must be painted or covered with roofing felt.

The construction, shown in separate diagrams, allows of outside nesting boxes with a lift-up lid. First make the two end frames to a vertical height of approximately 3 ft. 6 in. across the base. Join them with two 7 ft. 6 in. lengths each side, using halving joints. At one end arrange for a sliding door as shown, and fill in with boarding. At the other end form the nest boxes with 11 in. wide wood, the space will allow of three. Cover with a lid made in two pieces to hinge and overlap, and then fill in the upper portion. Join on the side lengths and, although not essential, the floor can be boarded, then fit the boards, and fit on a capping of 6 in. wide boards to leave a space for ventilation at the top.

The run is made with three 8 ft. lengths of $1\frac{1}{2}$ in. by $1\frac{1}{2}$ in. wood joined at the ends and in the centre with similar material. In one panel add a cross piece to form a door, this can be framed up from the same material. Hinge the door and then cover entirely with wire netting. The particular shape of the run allows for a waterproof cover to be laid over it in very wet weather. Paint the outside and limewash the inside.

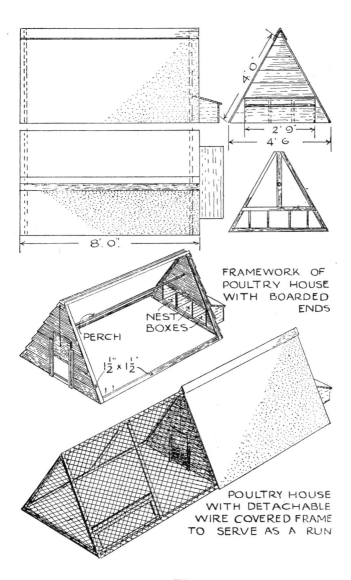

4' 0"

2' 9"

4' 6"

8' 0"

FRAMEWORK OF
POULTRY HOUSE
WITH BOARDED
ENDS

NEST
BOXES

PERCH

$1\frac{1}{2}" \times 1\frac{1}{2}"$

POULTRY HOUSE
WITH DETACHABLE
WIRE COVERED FRAME
TO SERVE AS A RUN

77

# RABBITS FOR FOOD

Rabbits form a valuable addition to the meat ration, they can be kept in a comparatively small space, and, to a great extent, fed on the waste products of the vegetable garden and such wild plants as dandelion, sow thistle, clover, groundsel, dried nettles, and chickweed. Part of their diet can consist of apple prunings, poplar twigs and leaves, cuttings from hawthorn and other deciduous trees as well as some of the refuse from the kitchen.

A suitable hutch for a beginning is shown on the next page. Provide a packing case about 3 ft. 6 in. by 1 ft. 6 in., as shown and bore holes for drainage in the bottom, as at A. Next fit in two pieces of 2 in. by 1 in. wood, as at B and C, the former being about 6 in. from the side and the latter about 12 in. On a line with the strip at C, fit a partition as at D to leave an opening of 6 in. or so. Fit frames of 2 in. by 1 in. or $1\frac{1}{2}$ in. by $\frac{3}{4}$ in. into the spaces formed at the ends by the uprights B and C, cover the former with thin boarding nailed on and the latter with wire netting, and then fill in the centre space with the same material.

The two framed doors should be hung with suitable hinges and fastened with turn buttons. Coat the inside with limewash and the outside with paint or distemper. If kept outside, cover with tarred felt or other roofing material.

Purchase the rabbits in the first place from a reliable breeder; addresses can be obtained from one of the weekly periodicals devoted to rabbits. Find out the kind of food and quantities that have been given to the rabbits previously and if possible keep to the same diet. Any changes in diet should be made gradually, especially from the root foods of the winter to the greenstuff of the spring. Special attention should be paid to regular cleansing of the hutch. Special leaflets dealing with rabbit keeping are issued free by the Ministry of Agriculture.

78

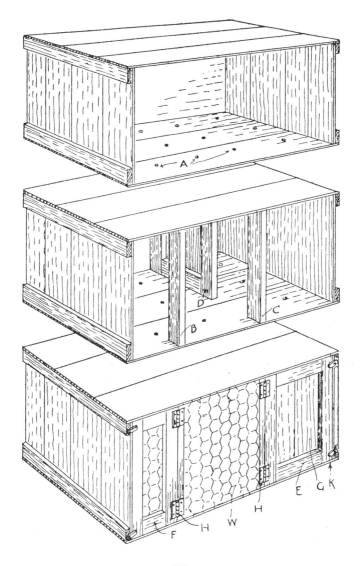

# MUSHROOM GROWING

The mushroom possesses a considerable food value, it includes a high rate of vitamens and a decided sugar content. Mushrooms can be grown all the year round in places where no other crops will grow, such as cellars, dark sheds, garages and even in spare rooms inside the house. They can be gathered from 8 to 10 weeks after the spawn has been planted, and will continue for two or three months.

Mushroom spawn is available in cartons of various sizes, No. 1 is sufficient to cover about 50 sq. ft. of compost, and is capable of producing upwards of $1\frac{1}{2}$ lbs. per sq. ft. The compost can be ordinary stable manure, but the disagreeable smell associated with farmyard manure can be entirely eliminated by the use of "Nomure," a scientifically produced substance, which, mixed with straw or chaff, forms a compost clean in use and odourless. It is spread over the straw or chaff, watered, turned over from time to time, and is ready in the course of two or three weeks.

For cultivation, provide a number of boxes to a convenient size having a depth of 6 in. or so, as shown at Fig. 1, page 81. The boxes can be arranged in tiers, as at Fig. 2, or in rows, as at Fig. 3. Portable trays, as at Fig. 3, are easily made. The compost should be spread on the trays to a depth of 5 in. and allowed to settle. The spawn is broken up and planted at intervals, and the compost covered with a thin layer of ordinary soil. An infrequent very light watering is applied, but never in sufficient quantity to seep through the boxes, and apart from keeping the beds free from weeds and away from draughts, no other attention is needed. When gathering the mushrooms, they are twisted from the bed—not cut —and the disturbed soil smoothed over. The stems are then cut off about $\frac{3}{4}$ in. from the cap. Spawn and "Nomure" can be obtained from the British Mushroom Industry, Ltd., Covent Garden Market, London, W.C.2.

PLATE XXXIII

MUSHROOM GROWING WITHOUT STABLE MANURE.

PLATE XXXIV

A GARDEN FRAME LIGHT
MADE FROM WINDOLITE.

GARDEN CLOCHES
EASILY MADE FROM WINDOLITE.

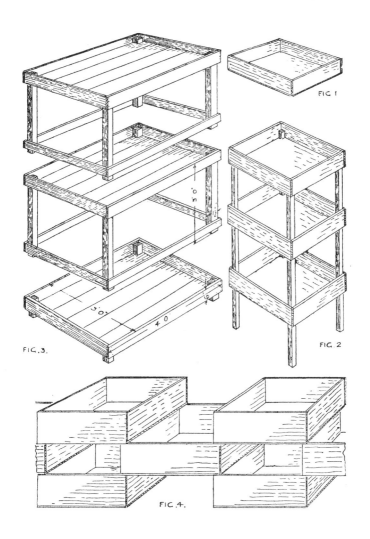

FIG 1

FIG 2

FIG.3.

FIG.4.

# THE GARDEN IN WAR TIME

The necessity for utilising all possible garden space for the growing of vegetables has already resulted in the loss of many small lawns and grass plots, and the uprooting of herbacious borders and flower beds, but even with the growing of the more prosaic but valuable vegetable, it is still possible to obtain decorative effects and include some of favourite flowers, which may be left in clumps here and there amidst green vegetables.

Instead of pleasing masses of colours, the gardener should aim at displays of foliage. The grass plot may well be dug up and utilised for potatoes and other root crop, but the old flower border offers opportunity for unusual planning. For example, try a border of carrots with cabbage lettuce behind. Further back, alternate ordinary and spinach beet with clumps of rhubarb and plants of ordinary and button tomatoes behind; the contrasts of colour being most effective. If there is room, an effective background can be provided by a row or two of brussels sprouts.

The extreme back of the border can be filled with main crop peas and runner beans, the latter being trained to sticks, with the peas growing on pea netting. Cabbages, savoys and kale can be grown between the rows of potatoes, and any ground occupied by early potatoes can be used for lettuce, crops of radish and onions. The possibilities of parsnips and turnips for root and tops should not be overlooked where space is available. Leeks can be grown easily and may be planted in clumps in the border.

The ground should be prepared as early as possible in the autumn or early winter. The turf from a lawn should be buried at least two spits deep or used for compost; in any case the soil should be piled up in high ridges to enable the frost to penetrate and destroy dormant grubs and wire-worm. Stable manure, if obtainable, is the best fertiliser for vegetables, but

PLATE XXXV

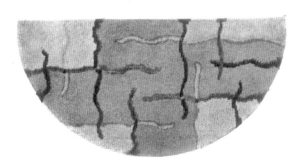

RUG DESIGNS.

failing it, use artificial manure. A seed bed will be needed and a frame or two will be invaluable in bringing up early lettuce, etc. The possibilities of cloches should be considered as an aid to raising early produce.

An important item, especially in war time, is the compost heap. All waste vegetable refuse, weeds, pea and bean haulms, waste leaves of all kinds, cabbage stalks, etc., should be piled together and treated with Adco, according to the directions supplied. In the course of time, the chemical action of Adco causes the waste to decay and provide a very valuable manure and dressing for the ground. If a pit can be dug in a corner of the garden and used for the purpose it is an advantage.

Tree and hedge prunings and old cabbage stalks should be burnt and the ashes used as a surface dressing, but as a rule, nothing should be burnt if it will decay in the compost heap.

One of the most important operations in the garden is to keep the surface of the soil free from weeds. Frequent hoeing is essential, not only to keep down weeds but to allow the soil to adsorb moisture. The fullest benefit from rain or watering cannot be obtained if the surface is allowed to get hard. The latter not only prevents proper aeration of the soil, but it encourages the growth of insects and protects them from their natural enemies—the birds.

With the opportunities that are developing for the acquisition of allotments, a much more ambitious scheme for growing vegetables is opened out. If the allotment is on grass land, some advice should be obtained as to the quality of the soil. Usually the agricultural department of the County Council will help in suggestions for the correct treatment. Allotment holders should obtain the leaflets issued by the Ministry of Agriculture and Fisheries, and should invest 3d. for the " Grow more Bulletin, No. 1." It is full of useful information as to soils, cultural operations, manuring, cropping, measures to control pests and diseases and storage.

# GARDEN FRAMES AND CLOCHES

The possibility of using a substitute for glass for covering garden frames and making cloches will appeal to the home gardener. The material suggested is called Windolite, it is a fraction of the weight of glass, it is unbreakable, admits ultra-violet rays, can be cut with a pair of scissors and is sold in rolls, 3 ft. wide, at 4s. 6d. a yard.

The diagrams at Fig. 1 show the construction of a garden light measuring 6 ft. 6 in. by 3 ft. 6 in., and Figs. 2 and 3 illustrate the method of making a frame. To make the light, take two lengths of batten, 5 ft. 10 in., 2 ft. 10 in. apart, as at A and B. Prepare four lengths 6 ft. 2 in. by 4 in. by $\frac{1}{2}$ in., and four 3 ft. 2 in. by 4 in. by $\frac{1}{2}$ in., place as shown at C and D. Tack a piece of Windolite first to one of the D pieces, allowing 1 in. for fastening. Next tack the material to the piece at the opposite end, stretching the material tight. Now take the sides in turn. Place the remaining battens to overlap the butt joints at the corners and then nail the pieces together.

The frame should be built up on corner pieces of $1\frac{1}{2}$ in. by $1\frac{1}{2}$ in. to 2 in. by 2 in., using stout boarding, at least $\frac{3}{4}$ in. Allow a slope of about 6 in., and provide a runner as at R in Fig. 3. If more convenient, the frame can be made to the full length of the light with a slope of about 3 in.

An all-light frame can be made for covering crops at ground level in the manner shown at Fig. 5. The length should be from 4 ft. to 3 ft. and the width from 3 ft. to 2 ft., with a height at the back of 18 in. and in front about 12 in. Windolite is tacked to the sides as well as the covering frame. The cloche shown at Fig. 6 is easily made by nailing strips of Windolite to suitable lengths of batten, it is economical to make the cloches to a length of 3 ft., which is the width of the material.

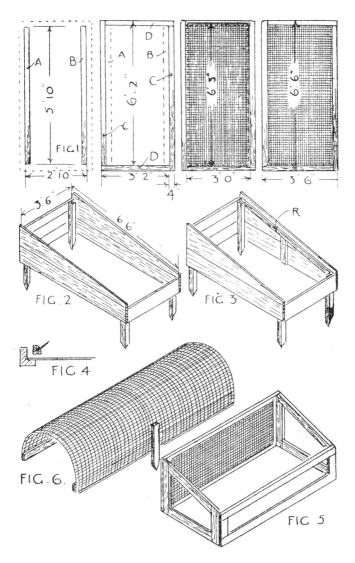

FIG 1

FIG. 2

FIC 3

FIC 4

FIG. 6.

FIG 5

85

# WINDOW BOXES

It is not generally realised that window boxes are just as suitable for growing lettuces as geraniums, and, with ordinary care and attention, a constant supply of greenstuff can be assured. The possessor of a garden need not bother about window gardening, unless it should be to supply flowers, but the dweller in a flat will find it very useful to grow the main materials for a salad.

The diagrams on the adjoining page illustrate the constructional features of two forms of window box. In both cases the material should be at least $\frac{3}{4}$ in. thick with strong joints at the corners. It will be seen that the front boards are deeper than those at the back, this is to allow for the fall or slope of the sill. Drainage holes should be bored in the bottom of the boxes, this is most important and should not be neglected. Notched joints are advised and, where possible, brass screws should be used in preference to iron screws or nails. The inside of the window box as well as the outside should be painted; hot pitch applied to the inside will render the window box almost everlasting. In order to prevent the drips after watering from disfiguring the wall or annoying any possible tenants underneath, the window boxes in upper flats should be provided with a zinc tray, as shown in a section on the next page.

A suggestion is given for the decorative treatment of a window box by means of applied slabs of thin wood. Suitably painted, the boxes will be as attractive as they are useful. The boxes should be filled first with a layer of broken crocks or coarse gravel and then with good quality potting mould. Lettuce plants should be grown from seed sown in shallow boxes inside the window and planted out when large enough. Begin in early spring, but it should be noted that protection from early frosts can be given by covering the boxes with glass, or with a cloche made with Windolite as shown on page 85.

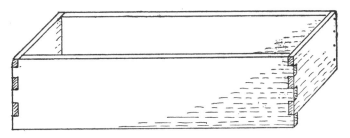

SIMPLE WINDOW·BOX

HOLES FOR DRAINAGE

ZINC TRAY TO PREVENT DRIPS

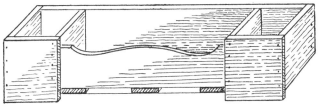

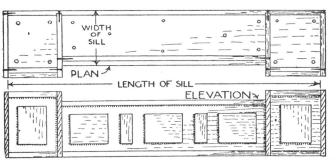

WIDTH OF SILL

PLAN

LENGTH OF SILL

ELEVATION

# THE PRODUCTION OF HONEY

Bee-keeping is a profitable occupation and in war-time it is especially useful owing to the considerable food value of honey, and its value in replacing sugar for many purposes. Bees are also active pollinators of fruit blossoms and render valuable assistance in the production of fruit. The prospective bee-keeper should obtain the latest leaflets on the subject from the Ministry of Agriculture and Fisheries.

Some care should be taken to provide a good stock and a properly constructed hive. Either a fully established stock or a swarm should be obtained for a beginning, but it should be noted that as bees are subject to disease, it is better to purchase a stock from a reliable bee-keeper, there are many addresses to be found in the agricultural papers.

If stocks are bought they should be obtained in the early spring, and locally if possible, and transferred to the new hive, preferably after sundown. At first it will be necessary to feed them with honey or sugar syrup, but as soon as they become climatised and used to their new home, they will start work. Feeding should commence in the late autumn and continued to the spring, remembering that bees store the honey to provide their own food during the winter.

Apart from the necessity of obtaining a really good stock of bees the most important part of bee-keeping is the hive, and unless it is made of good materials and soundly constructed, there is considerable risk of failure. A double walled hive is essential, for it must do more than contain its inhabitants, it must protect them from outside cold, draught and damp, and the interior must be easily accessible.

Hives should be placed in a sunny spot and sheltered from cold north and east winds, and as far away from the house as possible. Bees appear to dislike the close proximity of human beings, and should be left in peace.

# FIRST AID

A First Aid outfit should be considered as an essential part of the equipment of the home. Exactly how the outfit should be stored is a matter of individual convenience, but it should be placed where it is immediately available. A small cupboard or cabinet to hang on a wall, beyond the reach of young children, will be found generally convenient. The outfit should include an assortment of roller bandages from 1 in. to 3 in. wide, two or three triangular bandages, a packet each of ordinary and boracic lint, as well as adhesive tape, cotton wool and oiled silk. A pair of scissors, forceps, safety-pins, graduated medicine glass and a spoon or two. Arrange with clearly lettered labels, bottles containing iodine, sal-volatile, ammonia, ammoniated tincture of quinine, tincture of myrrh, castor oil and liniment. A number of small tins should contain vaseline, cold cream, antiseptic ointment, mustard, salt and boracic powder. A large tin of linseed meal and a dredger of ordinary flour should also be included, the latter for burns.

The necessary bandaging for fractures and sprains is illustrated on pages 91-97. Full notes on the treatment of fractures and sprains, as well as " ills " painful, illustrations will be found in " 101 Things for the Housewife to Do." First aid for the above injuries should only be applied by those having special knowledge. At least one member of the household should qualify for First Aid, most of the local authorities are providing classes for instruction.

As a rule, unless special knowledge of fractures is available, it is advisable not to move the patient if broken bones are suspected. The extent of the injury may be increased by unskilful treatment. This applies, in a lesser degree to severe sprains and before bandaging is attempted, it is always advisable to make sure that there is no dislocation or fracture. The application of splints should also be done by someone having had suitable training. If it should be essential that the patient must be moved before the arrival of skilled assistance, suspected fractures should be so supported that the least possible movement is made.

First aid for wounds consists in stopping the bleeding and in keeping the wound clean, using an antiseptic fluid, either a good proprietary brand or permanganate of potash dissolved in clean water. If the bleeding is in spurts and the blood is bright red, it is evident that an artery has been severed. In this case hold the limb up, apply pressure on the recognised pressure points and retain the pressure until the wound has been dressed. Nobody but a doctor or a person fully trained in First Aid should attempt to deal with serious wounds.

The treatment for shock should be carried out apart from any treatment for injury. Shock may be caused by a fall, by fright or any severe disturbance of the nervous system. The patient should be placed on the floor, on a bed or couch, and laid flat. Clothing should be loosened at the neck, chest and waist, to allow room for breathing. The patient should be covered with a rug and hot-water bottles placed at the feet and when able to drink, and on no account before, give hot drinks or, in summer, cold water.

The treatment for burns is to remove any clothing that does not adhere to the burn and keep away the air until the burn is dressed. Scalds and burns on which the skin has not been broken can be covered with flour, or dry lint, and lightly bandaged. If the burn is severe, it should be covered with tannic acid jelly. If the patient has been overcome by smoke and fumes, breathing can be restored by artificial respiration, but this should not be attempted without previous training. In severe cases it may be necessary to maintain artificial respiration for a long period and, therefore, should be carried out in relays.

# MAKING AND USING ROLLER BANDAGES

Roller bandages are made in various widths from cotton, linen, crêpe and flannel. Convenient widths are 1 in., $1\frac{1}{2}$ in. and 3 in., they are easily made from long strips of material wound on a roller made as shown on page 92.

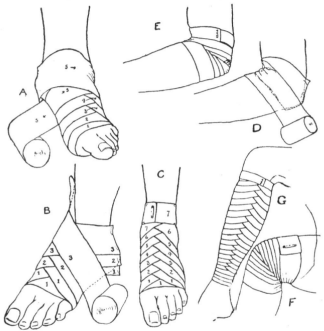

Three stages in using a roller bandage for sprained ankle are shown in stages at A, B and C. The first stage consists in wrapping a length of bandage round the upper part of the ankle, leaving about 6 in. free. Carry the bandage down to the little toe and round the foot under the ball of the big toe. Continue round again and carry the bandage round the heel, just below the ankle bone, leaving quite half the width projecting beyond the heel, as at A. Continue over the instep, as at B, and gradually work under the heel to well above the ankle as shown at C. Tie with a reef knot or pin.

The elbow and knee are similarly bandaged. Begin with a turn or two above the joint of the elbow, which should be flexed as at D. The next turn should be below the joint, the bandage covering the lower third of

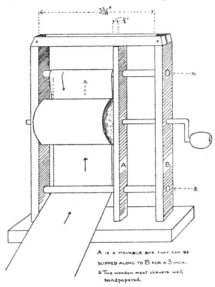

A IS A MOVABLE BAR THAT CAN BE
SLIPPED ALONG TO B FOR A 3 INCH.
✳ Two wooden meat skewers well
sandpapered.

the first turn. Continue round and carry the bandage above the point again so that the upper third of the first turn is covered. Continue in this way, first on one side and then on the other until sufficient of the elbow has been covered ; finish off as at E.

Allow plenty of room on each side of the knee-cap and keep the knee flexed during the binding. Finish with two turns, as at F, before the ends are tied or pinned, the latter method is to be preferred. In dealing with a leg bandage, as at G, begin above the ankle and finish below the knee.

# TRIANGULAR BANDAGES

The triangular bandage has a number of uses; it can be used as a sling or for the rapid bandaging of splints. The complete bandage is shown at A on the next page. The right angle at the top is called the apex, the lower corners, the ends, and the bottom edge, the base. The distance from the apex to the base should measure from 38 in. to 42 in.

The first fold is shown at B, and consists of placing the apex on line with the base. In the second fold at C, the upper edge is folded over to the base; this is known as the broad fold, the narrow fold is formed by bringing the upper edge to the base again (D).

The ends of the bandage should be tied with the reef knot, as shown in stages at A, B, C, D, E and F. Two methods of using the bandage are shown, the small arm sling (F) is used for fractures and injuries to the forearm and hand; for injuries to the upper arm, use the large sling (E). For securing splints, use either the broad or narrow folds.

## HAND AND FINGER BANDAGING

The illustrations on page 96 show the stages in bandaging the thumb, finger, hand and the method to be used to stop bleeding while a cut is being treated. In dealing with the thumb, begin with a turn or two round the wrist, leaving a few inches of the bandage free. Bring the bandage as far down the thumb as it is necessary to cover and give a complete turn as at A. Carry the bandage over the back of the hand, give it a turn round the wrist and back over to the thumb as shown at B. Continue as shown at C until the thumb is covered up to the wrist and finish off by tying to the free end or fasten with a safety pin.

In dealing with a finger bandage, begin with a turn or two round the wrist, and then carry the bandage

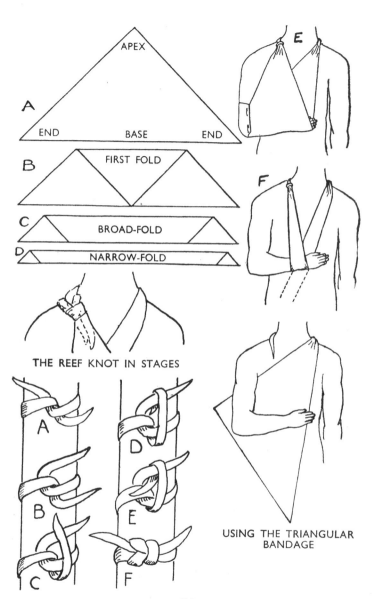

A  APEX  END  BASE  END

B  FIRST FOLD

C  BROAD-FOLD

D  NARROW-FOLD

E

F

THE REEF KNOT IN STAGES

A

B

C

D

E

F

USING THE TRIANGULAR BANDAGE

down to the particular finger. To fix a dressing below the first joint carry over the bandage as at D, wrap round the finger and bring up and either tie or pin. In case of an injury to the finger tip, fold as indicated at E, and finish as indicated at G.

For bandaging the whole hand, the method shown in stages at G, H and K is advised. Begin with a turn or two round the wrist, carry down to the fingers with a complete turn as at G. Bring up to above the thumb, which can be left free, carry behind and then down, under the fingers and back again, and continue three or four times when the bandage is finished off as at K.

These diagrams of bandaging are largely based on a selection of those comprised in the two excellent handbooks by Mr. William E. Bradford, Instructor to the City of London Red Cross Society, 1915–17, entitled "First-Aid Bandaging" and "The Roller Bandage." They each contain a comprehensive series of admirably clear diagrams which will be found essential to all taking up first aid work. They are published by Messrs. George Allen & Unwin, at 1s. net and 1s. 6d. net respectively.

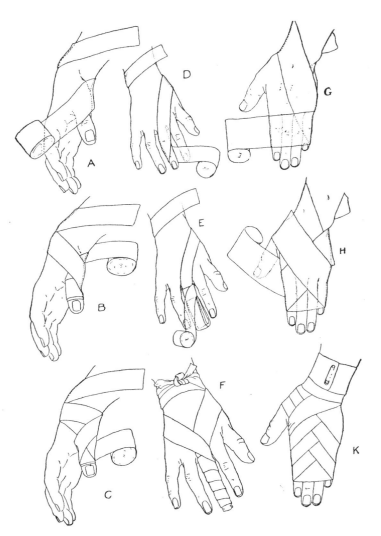

BANDAGING THE HAND AND FINGERS

# SPLINTS

Splints can be obtained in a number of shapes and sizes, but they can be made at home by the handyman. Although any light wood can be used, the best material is Balsa, which is remarkably light and quite strong enough for ordinary purposes. For general use, splints for the finger, arms and legs will be found useful. Two kinds of splint are shown for use with finger injuries, the straight shape at G is not so useful as the curved splint at H, the shape should be formed with suitable planes. A plain arm splint is shown at K, the length may vary from 14 in. to 16 in. Although the curved arm splint at L is more difficult to make it is generally preferred. The leg splint at N is used for lower leg injuries, the small hole at the bottom allows for the ankle bone. A plain inside leg splint is shown at M. In all cases the surfaces of splints should be perfectly smooth.

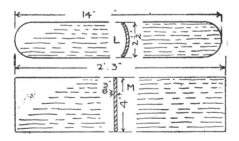

# SAVING FUEL

With the rationing of fuel, gas and electricity, economy must be exercised, but as many housewives are normally careful it is not a simple matter to further reduce consumption. Warm rooms in winter are essential to comfort, meals must be cooked and the long winter evenings demand bright and cheerful lighting.

Coal may be economised in various ways, one way being to use the largest room as a general living-room and keep up one fire instead of two or more. With gas or electric fires in other rooms, a minimum of heating can be supplied just when needed. Bowl fires will be found of value as the heat rays can be directed to any desired position.

Coal fires can be kept going by using coke, and when not required to give out a lot of heat they can be banked down with coal dust. All the coal dust in the cellar or bin should be piled up on one side and kept for this purpose or made into briquettes. The latter can be made by mixing together one part of coal tar pitch to nine parts of coal dust, heated over a fire. The mixture can be poured into moulds formed by cardboard boxes. If clay is available, use the same proportions, but in this case the mixture can be moulded into balls and left to dry. Prepared coal in the form of Coalite is economical, and it will be found that the installation of an anthracite stove will give continuous heat at a lower cost than a large open fire.

It is important to conserve heat as much as possible, draughts should be reduced to a minimum, doors should be kept shut and preferably curtained. If a domestic boiler is used for a hot water system, the use of anthracite will be found quite as economical as coke and far less trouble as it is not so liable to clinker. The hot water tank should be jacketed, a simple method being to wrap it up in boiler felt or pieces of old carpet, or to make a case of wood from old packing cases or plywood, to allow of space of several inches all round, to be filled with sawdust, chaff or other material. The hot water tank treated in this way will keep hot for considerable periods. Exposed hot water pipes may also be covered with strips of felt.

In using electric fires, the number of elements should be reduced as soon as the room is warm. The burners of a gas fire should be kept free from dust and any broken radients replaced at the earliest opportunity.

Heat for cooking can be conserved by using cleaned kettles and saucepans; carbon deposits on the bottom of these utensils retard the heat. Do not allow the gas to flare up round the sides of utensils. An iron plate on the top of the gas cooker will enable several saucepans to be used with one gas ring. The gas rings should be kept quite clean and the inside of the oven spotless. Arrange for as much cooking to be done as possible at one time and endeavour to turn off the gas early enough to allow the heat in the oven to complete the cooking.

The use of steam should be considered as a cooking economy, two- or three-tier steamers can be used to cook a whole meal. Waterless and pressure cookers are most economical in use and, considering the saving in fuel, they are not expensive. There are several forms of cooker on the market in which meat, fish, vegetables and a pudding can be cooked at one time.

Logs serve to save coal and give out great heat, but they should be quite dry. Branches of trees, twigs of all kinds, pine needles and cones, etc., should be collected when they are available. If peat is obtainable it is excellent for fires and dead leaves may be gathered and mixed with coal dust and clay to make briquettes.

The weekly consumption of fuel, gas and electricity should be carefully checked and the regular reading of the meters should be recorded so that consumption can be regulated.

# LAMP SHADES FOR THE BLACK-OUT

Unless windows are heavily curtained with suitable pelmets small beams of light may escape through the crevices at the top or through the sides of the blinds. Suggestions are given on page 104 for various means of masking the light in a room, but if it is inconvenient to use opaque masking, it will be necessary to provide some means of preventing the reflected light from the ceiling and direct rays from the lamp showing outside.

An effective shape is shown at A. It is intended to throw the light downwards and forwards across the room. The large circular top prevents the light shining directly on the ceiling. The shade can be made of stiff cardboard or strawboard to any convenient size, the diameter of the top may be any size from 8 in. to 12 in. The internal diameter of the shade should be about 6 in. and the depth of the shade from 9 in. to 12 in. The method of construction is shown at B and C, the projections on the top of the upright surround should correspond with the slits in the circular top.

Any ordinary lampshade may be made more effective for black-out purposes by providing a circular cover, allowing an air space underneath. Slight shading can be provided by a pleated cover made from crêpe paper. With even one thickness of crêpe paper, especially if black, a pleated shade is quite effective. This particular shade is easily made by taking a long strip from 6 in. to 12 in. wide, pleating it at intervals of $\frac{1}{2}$ in. and running a thread through the complete thickness about 1 in. from one end. Tie the ends of the thread after spreading out in fan shape.

Another effective shade for covering the existing shape to prevent ceiling rays is shown at D. A circular shape is cut out as shown at E, the angle of the cut depends on the amount of splay needed ; it is intended that the new shade should rest on the top of the existing one.

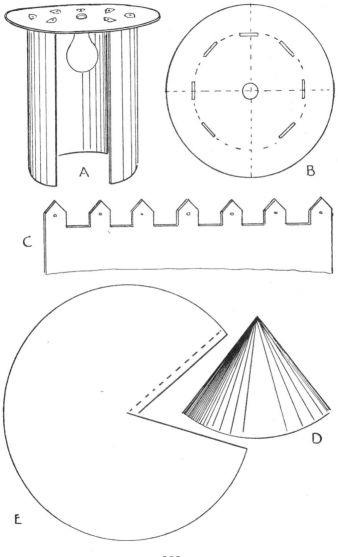

A

B

C

D

E

101

# PROTECTION FROM SPLINTERING GLASS

It is certainly advisable in certain areas to provide protection from splintering glass. Even if glass windows are covered by boards, either inside or outside the room, it is impossible to avoid breakage entirely, as the pressure on the air caused by a powerful explosive will shatter the glass in any shuttered windows. The danger comes from the flying splinters.

One of the general methods of masking windows is to fit plywood sheets to the inside framework and keep them in position by means of turn-buttons. Window masking by this method is effective in so far as the total obliteration of light is concerned, but at the best it is a troublesome job, not only to put up the shields and take them down, but to store them during the day. By far the most satisfactory method is to use blinds of stout material together with heavy curtains, with the latter it is possible to keep the windows open for ventilation.

One of the ways of protecting against flying splinters is to provide a frame to fit inside the window and cover it with wire netting, the frame should be removable for window cleaning. One of the recommended methods of protection is to strengthen the glass by means of paper strips glued directly to the surface. Gummed paper strip about 1 in. wide is admirable for the purpose, the tape used for wrapping paper can be used, it is available in several colours. A better material, although slightly more expensive, is *passe-partout* binding. Unless it is carefully done the strips give an untidy appearance. Several suggestions are given on the next page for patterned effects by paper strips. As far as possible the strips should be closer together in the centre of the window; there is not so much danger from splinters from the edges of the glass which are firmly bedded in putty. Another method of giving protection is to cover the glass completely with transparent cellulose sheets or with window transparencies imitating stained glass.

# WINDOW MASKING

The emergency caused by the war necessitated immediate masking of all windows, and this, in most cases, called for temporary expedients. As it may be necessary to continue the masking over an extended period, methods should be devised to save labour and yet be thoroughly effective.

The most satisfactory method for preventing inside lighting being visible from the outside of the house is to use opaque blinds and comparatively light-proof curtains. Even with well-fitting blinds, light may filter through the top of the window unless protected by a pelmet, the latter may be attached to the top sash as at Fig. 1. So that the window can be opened, the material used, canvas, American cloth, or any other suitable fabric, should be tacked to the frame as at Fig. 2.

When the blinds are narrow, there is a risk of light showing at the edges of the window, this can be obviated by fastening strips of strawboard or thin plywood at the sides, as shown at Fig. 3. If the window frame will allow the strips to be fastened on so that the blind runs inside, it will be more satisfactory. An alternative method is to paint the glass for a distance of 3 in. or so ; this is shown at Fig. 6.

Pelmet supports are not only useful for top protection, but also for hanging heavy curtains, using runners as indicated at Fig. 4. Suitable strips of wood should be provided to fit across the top of the frame and secured with angle brackets, as shown at Fig. 5. With a deep pelmet and lined curtains there will be no need for blinds.

For windows which are not fitted with blinds, and in places where curtains are not practicable, it may be advisable to use a fabric-covered frame made to fit inside the window opening. A suitable frame for the purpose is shown at Fig. 7. The material need not be more than $1\frac{1}{2}$ in. by $\frac{3}{4}$ in. and the covering of hessian, coated thickly with distemper.

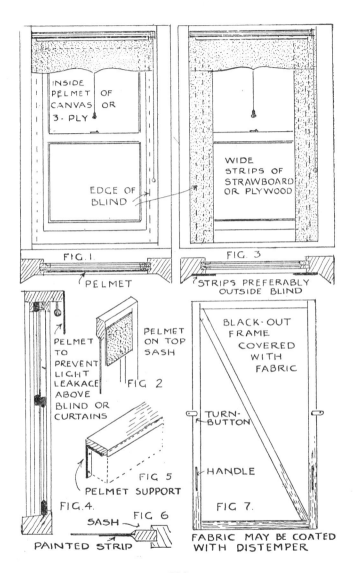

FIG. 1

INSIDE PELMET OF CANVAS OR 3-PLY

EDGE OF BLIND

PELMET

FIG. 3

WIDE STRIPS OF STRAWBOARD OR PLYWOOD

STRIPS PREFERABLY OUTSIDE BLIND

PELMET TO PREVENT LIGHT LEAKAGE ABOVE BLIND OR CURTAINS

FIG.4.

PELMET ON TOP SASH

FIG 2

FIG 5

PELMET SUPPORT

FIG 6

SASH

PAINTED STRIP

BLACK-OUT FRAME COVERED WITH FABRIC

TURN-BUTTON

HANDLE

FIG 7.

FABRIC MAY BE COATED WITH DISTEMPER

# WINDOW VENTILATION DURING BLACK-OUT

In small rooms especially, it is necessary to provide for ventilation and, unless this is provided by ventilators fixed in the wall, it should be arranged by opening the window ; this, however, must be done without interference with the masking.

The simplest method of providing for a current of air is shown on the next page at A, and consists of raising the lower sash to leave a space between the upper and lower sashes. The open space under the bottom sash should be filled in with a block of wood or a frame covered with plywood. Metal casement windows can be kept open and secured by the stay, or by the notches in the handle.

A more effective form of ventilation can be arranged by fitting a framework on the top sash, the opening being filled with louvre boards, as indicated at B. In this case there is ventilation at two points, as there is an opening between the two sashes. The framework should be from 9 in. to 12 in. deep and the whole length of the sash. The number of louvre boards will depend on the depth, but they must overlap sufficiently to prevent direct rays escaping. With opaque blinds and heavy curtains it is not essential that the above fittings should be provided, but in windy weather they will prevent the blinds and curtains from blowing out.

Fabric or plywood covered screens intended to cover the window completely can be provided with openings to allow of a free current of air, a simple method being shown at C and D. The top of the framework should project 2 in. or more, and leave an opening of from 6 in. to 12 in., depending on the size of the frame. This opening should be covered and overhang the opening for several inches, at least one-third more than the depth of the opening. The sides should be filled in and the inside blackened to prevent light escaping.

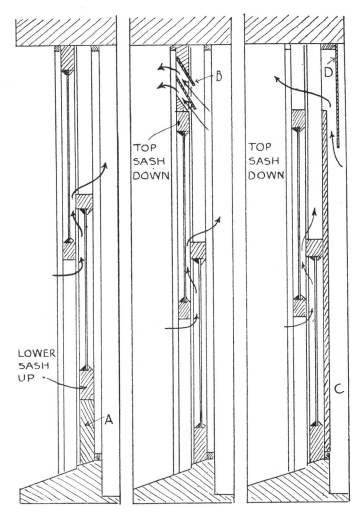

B

TOP
SASH
DOWN

D

TOP
SASH
DOWN

LOWER
SASH
UP

A

C

FRAME OR
BLOCK OF WOOD
UNDER SASH

FRAME WITH
LOUVRE BOARDS
ON TOP SASH

MASKING FRAME
WITH SHIELD
OVER OPENING

# CASES FOR GAS MASKS

Protection must be provided for the cardboard container issued by the A.R.P. authorities if, as advised, it is to be available at any time. Although the box is made of stout strawboard, it will soon drop to pieces if allowed to get very wet. One method of protection is to coat the strawboard with size and then apply a couple of coats of varnish or paint. In addition it is certainly advisable to provide a case which should be made of waterproof material.

White American and Lancaster cloth are particularly effective and comparatively inexpensive materials. Willesden canvas is suitable for heavy wear, but leather is the most durable although more costly. Glazed calico is another suitable material.

Cases are easily made with thin material, and the diagram on the next page illustrates the method of measuring up and cutting out. As there is some slight variation in dimensions, check up the given sizes. Allow at least $\frac{1}{4}$ in. for turnings, the same amount being left for a hem on the flap. Bind the top and flap with suitable binding, as shown in the sketch.

The shoulder strap may be made of bias binding or strips of the cloth suitably hemmed as shown, it can be made in one length or cut into two lengths with a pronged buckle, the latter should not be so placed that it rests on the shoulder. The case can be fastened with a button and a buttonhole slit worked on a suitable length of binding, or with a press fastener, as indicated.

Another form of case can be made to hold a gas mask without the rectangular cardboard box, it should be made from one of the materials stated above, cut out to the shape shown in the diagram at the bottom of the next page. No allowance is shown for turnings, otherwise the work will be found quite straightforward. The shoulder strap should be attached to the top of the case.

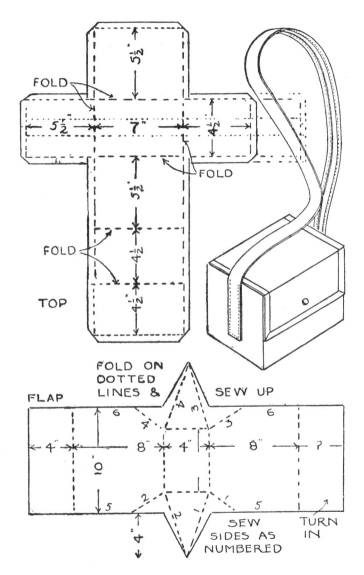

FOLD

$5\frac{1}{2}$

FOLD

$5\frac{1}{2}"$    7"    $4\frac{1}{2}$

FOLD

$5\frac{1}{2}"$

FOLD

$4\frac{1}{2}"$

$4\frac{1}{2}"$

TOP

FOLD ON
DOTTED
LINES &

SEW UP

FLAP

6    4   3    6

4      3

← 4" →|← 8" →|← 4" →|← 8" →|← 7

10"

5

2   1    5

2

4"

SEW
SIDES AS
NUMBERED

TURN
IN

109

# ECONOMISING ARTIFICIAL LIGHT

The problem of obtaining a maximum of lighting with a minimum of consumption is one confronting all householders during war time, and the long hours of black-out. As a rule, light should be concentrated just where it is required most of all. In places such as entrance halls, passages, bedrooms, the lighting may be dimmed, but in the living-rooms, the aim should be good lighting without glare.

In an ordinary house there may be two rooms where the lighting should be good and impart a feeling of cheerfulness, and in this case special care must be taken that it is obscured from outside view. One good lamp of 100 watts should be suspended in the centre of the room, and covered by a large and shallow conical shade, designed to illuminate the whole of the floor space and not the ceiling. A table under the light would be sufficiently illuminated for handicrafts or table games. Standards, with 60 c.p. bulbs and a similar top shade will be found useful in places where additional light is needed or when the larger light is not required.

The light from low-wattage lamps can be considerably increased by fitting reflector shades. Reflection from ordinary opaque or semi-opaque shades is easily effected by covering the inside with white paper or coating it with white paint. Blue bulbs with a small transparent circle underneath are useful for passages, bathrooms, etc.

A most economical form of lighting is paraffin, and readers who live in vulnerable areas should have one or two such lamps for use in the event of a failure in the electrical supply. The vapour type of paraffin lamp gives a far more brilliant light than the wick burning kind. The range of the lamps known as " Aladdin " will be found most effective, and are available for use on the table, but for greater safety should be of the suspension type.

# EVACUEES

The present billeting allowance for lodging an unaccompanied child is 10s. 6d., and for each child more than one, 8s. 6d. This covers full board, lodging and care. For each adult accompanying a child, 5s., and for each child (under five) accompanied by an adult, 3s. ; this covers lodging only with provision for water, cooking, etc. Adults with young children with them are expected to pay for their own food, and if unable to do this should obtain assistance from the local authority.

Householders who have serious complaints to make against billeting arrangements or evacuees may appeal to a special tribunal to be set up by the local authority, but otherwise they are expected to keep to the terms of their agreement or the conditions imposed on them by compulsory powers. It is understood that claims for damage caused by evacuees will be considered at the expiration of the war.

Many householders, especially in homes where there are no children, find the responsibility of feeding and of the care of young children brings considerable anxiety, and more so when educational facilities are wanting. It is often difficult to keep them out of mischief, especially when they come from homes where the discipline is lax. Much of the difficulty may be overcome by laying down a few simple rules, but it is quite essential to their success that they should be enforced. Kindness, unless backed up by firmness, is likely to lead to undue advantages being taken.

Much can be done by joining with neighbours in a similar position to provide entertainment and in making up parties for recreation and walks under the supervision of householders in turn. The children should be encouraged to help with the household duties, boys as well as girls should be expected to take their turn. During the long evenings, especially on dark nights when it is difficult to walk about, the children should be encouraged to take up a simple hobby. " 101 Things for Little Folks to Do " is full of suggestions.

Another of the difficulties likely to be experienced is that of catering in order to keep the cost down to the small amount allowed. As a rule, children have healthy appetites especially when they have been moved from congested areas to the pure air of country or seaside.

Several pages have been devoted to suggestions for economical dishes and all of them will be found useful in providing satisfying and economical meals. The house-keeper should watch prices and adapt requirements to the state of the market.

A careful watch must be kept to prevent waste of any kind. It should not be necessary to economise by reducing the quantity of food although the quality may not be so good, but the economy should be exercised in using every scrap of food to the best advantage, in making it yield the utmost nourishment.

Children are usually able to digest plenty of starchy foods such as potatoes and bread. Butter beans, peas and lentils provide a satisfying addition to a meal and the value of root vegetables, such as swedes, turnips, carrots and Jerusalem artichokes should not be forgotten.

Many children do not care greatly for fish, but when made in the form of fish pies, it is usually relished. Scraps of left-over fish pounded and mixed with a little margarine and a drop or two of anchovy essence make an appetising spread for toast buttered with margarine.

Milk puddings made with condensed milk, toad in the hole with beef sausages and plain batter, potato cakes made with left-over potatoes, steamed green vegetables and minced meat, and similar cakes made with boiled rice with added vegetables, minced meat and flavoured with sauce are all very economical dishes, easily prepared and usually welcomed.

Any scarcity of sugar which is a necessity for growing children, can be made up with treacle, honey and sweet fruits such as dates.

# LET US TIDY UP *

One of the most helpful of the 101 things to be done, especially in war-time, is the cultivation of habits of tidiness not only in our own homes, but in the streets and countryside. It is a blot on our civilisation that litter is strewn about in the streets, country roads, on commons and open spaces, and it is a reproach that many of us do so little to rectify a common failing.

It is in the home that habits of tidiness should be formed, and there is much to be done with children from their early years that will have effect in later life. Children should be encouraged to pack their toys away neatly at the end of the day, suitable receptacles being provided and used only for that purpose. Children attending school should have some place allocated for school books, and cupboards or shelves for storing games and hobbies.

The long evenings of the black-out provide opportunities for the more convenient re-arrangement of cupboards, shelves and drawers, etc. Additional shelves can be fitted in cupboards so that the contents can be quickly found. Waste space in the house can be put to better use, and, as far as possible, a definite place should be found for everything in everyday use. A waste-paper basket or box should be placed in every room, and instead of burning paper, save it for collection.

The handyman may make himself useful by providing extra cupboard room in recesses, additional hooks in wardrobes and behind doors, etc., by making racks to hold the household brooms and brushes, and by making divisions in table and other drawers. The possibility of utilising the waste space under the kitchen table or under the sink, by making cupboards to hold kitchen utensils should not be overlooked. The extra storing space will be appreciated by the housewife and make the job of keeping things tidy much easier.

* With acknowledgments to The Dryad Press.

# INDEX

The figures in Roman type refer to the photographic illustrations,
and those in Italic refer to the drawings in the text.

114

# INDEX

# INDEX

116

# INDEX

# NOTES